THE
INSTANT

Also by Amy Liptrot

The Outrun

THE
INSTANT
AMY LIPTROT

CANONGATE

First published in Great Britain in 2022
by Canongate Books Ltd, 14 High Street, Edinburgh EH1 1TE

canongate.co.uk

1

British Library Cataloguing-in-Publication Data
A catalogue record for this book is available on
request from the British Library

ISBN 978 1 83885 426 3
Export ISBN 978 1 83885 427 0

Typeset in Bembo Std by Palimpsest Book Production Ltd,
Falkirk, Stirlingshire

Printed and bound in Great Britain by Clays Ltd, Elcograf S.p.A.

MIX
Paper from
responsible sources
FSC
www.fsc.org   FSC® C018072

For the Heartsick

CONTENTS

PROLOGUE

February
Hunger Moon

I'VE BEEN GETTING TEXT MESSAGES from the moon. A note flashes on my phone, asking if the moon can track my location, and I consent.

I have moved to a new city but the moon is following me around. It texts to tell me when it will be out. Through the windows of my flat in Kreuzberg, there is just a parallelogram of sky at the top of the courtyard, only a small space to catch the passing moon on certain clear nights.

B said that people move here just so they can tell their friends back home that they're living in Berlin. B said that people moving here often feel like they've dropped several years, that they can extend their youth.

The app uses my location to tell me the moon's phase, direction, distance at all times. Right now, the moon is 384,012 miles away from my hand, which is holding my phone close to my heart, as I sit at the table in the narrow kitchen of this flat with tall windows in an old-style apartment block, stinging nettles by the front door. I'm just home from work, vibrating with tiredness. The moon is waxing gibbous and is 25.2 degrees above the horizon, almost due east. It rose just after midday and will set around 3 a.m.

I run a bath, consult my digital charts, then wait for the moon. My bath is next to the window and I open it wide to the cool air. I hear stray cats mewing in the stairwell, magpies rattling in the bare trees and the indistinct rumble of the city that reminds me of the wind back home. My first sight of the moon is its reflection in my opposite neighbour's window: a bulbous glow in a double-glazed mirror. Over the evening, it passes like a distant ship. I keep going back to the window and am thrilled to catch its oblivious light.

In the stairwell there are political graffiti and signs: anti-gentrification, pro-refugee, anarchist. The building used to be squatted and there are some communal elements between the flats: shared Wi-Fi and handyman. I hear the neighbours around the courtyard, sex and arguments in various languages, someone playing the flute, a baby crying. Every 1 May, there is a big techno party in the courtyard. It's electric around here.

The internet is hectic and I go to the moon to relax, opening new browser tabs for the moon's Wikipedia page and Google Maps of its surface. I follow new lunar developments from NASA. I learn that the moon was probably once part of the earth, sheared off by an asteroid. B, who moved from Scotland to Tasmania, tells me that there is a different moon in the southern hemisphere: it waxes and wanes in the opposite direction. I learn that the moon is slowing down the earth's rotation. The moon is holding on to us.

I grew more aware of the moon and, in particular, its effect on the tides when I was back home on the island. Low tide at new moon is the time to dig for shellfish called spoots on the beach, and after a full moon is the time to go looking for things washed up – driftwood and treasure – at the high-water line.

★   ★   ★

My street and the few surrounding are a mix between different eras of Kreuzberg: corner shops, Turkish bakeries, a garage selling 'revolution equipment', next to a sushi place, high-concept coffee shops and designer boutiques. There are clothes piled on the pavement for anyone to take for free and there are also places selling dresses for a thousand euros.

People on the internet ask questions. What is the moon made of? Why can I see the moon during the day? Why is the moon red? Can the moon be destroyed?

I've been wearing long skirts and fingerless gloves, painting my nails like I used to. I've been going to parties. In the English-language bookshop, I read aloud from *The Odyssey* while two Norwegians played synth.

I've run away but I find the moon everywhere I go. I found a tiny pink plastic crescent in Tempelhofer Feld – a huge park in the middle of the city – right there on the footpath. In my first week in the city I found a beautiful lunar calendar in a bookshop and have it Blu-tacked to my wall. Twice a month at new and full moon I await Syzygy: the instant when moon, earth and sun are aligned. The lunar cycles are almost all I have in my diary for the year. My future is blank but I know what the moon will be doing.

There will be thirteen full moons in the coming

solar calendar year. The full moons of each month and season have different traditional names. February's full moon is the Hunger Moon and March's is known as the Lenten, Worm or Sap Moon. The names come to us from various cultures – Native American, Celtic, Anglo-Saxon – but are all tied to the seasons and agricultural year.

The moon has now passed over the courtyard and behind the buildings but I'm looking at photographs of it online. I close Twitter, the dating app, the eBay listings. Lunar mosaics are created by hundreds of different image frames taken through a telescopic camera, added together to create a highly detailed picture of the moon's surface: textured craters, mountains and cliffs. They are magnified, monochrome and glowing. It's February, and the city is dim but I'm madly seeking moonlight.

I've been in Berlin for four months and have lived in five houses. I've been cycling over cobbles. I've been keeping my devices charged, wearing shorts I found on the pavement. I've been sitting outside *Spätis* corner-shops, smoking roll-ups, drinking Club-Mate, watching attractive and strange people on the street. I had a love affair that lasted for two nights and two afternoons.

People in this town can't commit to anything, but the moon is always orbiting and the months pass relentlessly. I don't speak the language but I know '*der Mond*'.

My attachment to the moon grew during the years I've been lonely and so did the moon's attachment to me. The moon, I tell B, is my boyfriend.

6

HOW TO SWIM THROUGH WAVES

July
Thunder Moon

L AST SUMMER I RENTED A little flat on the island, in the small harbour town, close enough to the pier to hear the passenger announcements on the ferry, which arrived twice a day, its horn setting a slow rhythm to the days.

I had ripped up a redundant London *A–Z* and used the pages as wallpaper. My shower was full of sand and seaweed.

Outside the back door, where I went to smoke, chittering sparrows filled the ivy. I was picking up bits of work, considering another season with my old employers, waiting for something to happen.

Although I had this place now, with a bookshelf and

broadband, I often found myself standing in the kitchen awash with loneliness. I'd been living alone for a few years and it was getting to me.

Often I'd walk to the top of the hill and watch the moon rise. I'd look down over the town and out across the bay to the other islands and, beyond, to mainland Scotland and out west where the Atlantic stretches.

On other nights, I stayed up late travelling in bed, wandering the internet. With my laptop whirring warmly on my duvet, I walked the streets of international cities with Google Street View.

I fall asleep. I dream I am a bird flying high above the internet.

Once a week or so, I met my eccentric sea-swimming group. We chatted while getting undressed beside our cars, about the weather, sea temperature and conditions. Then, without too much hesitation, we'd walk together into the water.

I also swam alone, often from a small beach at the edge of town. I'd eye the water doubtfully for a while before peeling off my jeans and feeling the wind cold on my legs. I put on my swim boots and gloves and left the rest of my clothes piled up on the pebbles. I moved into the water in increments, all my pores and organs and bodily functions reacting to the cold immersion. When the water was at the bottom of my ribcage, I gathered my will and pushed off into breaststroke, gasping aloud.

These were the best minutes of my week. I swam parallel with the coast, getting used to the temperature, my limbs pale under the greenish water, some sea in my mouth, never going too far out or staying in too long. For those minutes I submitted to the sea, to being submerged to the neck and trusting I would be held up.

The sea was the only place where I didn't take my phone. Most nights I spent my evenings scrolling. I got stuck on an oddly translated Wiki-how page about 'how to swim through waves'.

The easiest way to let a wave pass is to duck under it.

I took a trip south, travelling the country, staying with couples, hearing them chat and laugh through the wall at night. When I came back to the island, I was in a filthy mood, angry, contained and dissatisfied.

I was sexually frustrated and my heart ached. I wanted to cry and often did. For the first time in my life, I felt aware of myself ageing, my thirties speeding by. I was embarrassed by my conventional desires. I had hoped I was more resourceful and interesting than to want a boyfriend. But the moon, cold and elusive, was not always enough.

I downloaded Tinder and its location-based algorithm showed me inaccessible people on oil rigs and passing fishing boats far out to sea.

If you see an exceptionally big wave approaching, the best method is to swim straight towards it.

I developed a crush on a friend and after some time found the courage to tell him. Politely but firmly, he said he wasn't interested. Boundless sadness. I was ashamed to be so upset over something that hadn't happened, to be upset over nothing. I raised and destroyed armies in my mind.

I decided to make myself get over it. I would seduce someone else I knew. I shaved my legs, put on a dress and walked to his house. He wasn't in. After that, I didn't have it in me. I wasn't too bothered.

Island gigantism is the phenomenon by which animals constrained to an island become, over generations, larger than animals of the same species on the mainland. Without as many predators or competitors, they are able to evolve to be bigger. It's most commonly seen in rodents. On my islands, voles and mice have been shown to be bigger than their cousins on the mainland.

If you find yourself caught by a wave and tumbled around, relax! Don't try to fight it. The wave will let you go in a few seconds.

I walked up the Black Craig, then along the lonely stretch of coast to the highest cliffs on the island. From the coastal path, I looked at the wave-energy devices bobbing on the sea and waved to the ferry but I don't think anyone waved back. A sea stack looked like a colossal exclamation mark dropped into the water, an improbable structure that I imagined collapsing right then and there with only me watching. I thought about how, the day before in the supermarket fruit-and-veg aisle holding a soggy lettuce, I decided I was definitely leaving the island at the end of the summer, but right now, up there with the pink thrift and orchids and lapwings and wheatears and puffins, I didn't feel so sure.

I thought about how someone had told me there is only one house on the island that can't be seen from another. I thought about how the tiny *Primula scotica* likes exposed salty places.

I followed the burn up into the hills to find a wooden sauna I'd heard about and seen pictures of, taken not so long ago. Curlews were going bonkers. I found the little waterfall and the pool dammed up below it but the sauna wasn't there. It had burned to the ground, leaving only blackened stumps. I cooled my feet in the water, walked to the road, then hitched a lift back to town with a seal biologist.

I had the skeleton of a good life but there was no heart inside. I'd been wearing the same warm layers year round for the last two years. My summer and party dresses hung in the wardrobe unworn. My photos used to be all of people; now they were of the sky.

The birds I saw were the high point of my day. One day, a male harrier, a silver glimpse while driving; the next, a pair of eider ducks in the harbour, cooing comically.

I was living midway between my parents and in the middle of their communications. Divorced a decade earlier, they used me to find out information about the other.

I tried to be okay, to relax and be grateful for what I had, but I kept being jolted by a lurching for more.

The same desire and self-belief that motivated me made me frustrated. The pain was a by-product of my ambition.

If you find yourself getting beat-up by the waves, you either need to go into the shallower water, or get away from the shore past the waves.

There were days when the loneliness built up and came spilling out in angry comments – often directed at the island. On nights when I was aching and alone, I wondered if this was the life I'd stopped drinking to live.

I needed to get away. I wanted an adult life, restaurants, sexiness, conversation and art. I wanted to meet new people who didn't know old things about me.

I got paid and had enough in my bank account to see me through a few months so decided to set sail. I gave notice on the lease of my flat and, in barely any time, got up early one morning to board the ferry.

I've always loved how it feels to leave: the motion of the ferry pulling away from the pier and the island, the bus setting off down the A9.

As Scotland passes, in my notebook, my dream diary, I write to the great love of my future, imagining lines and declarations to a faceless, nameless fantasy:

I want to sleep in every room of your house.
I want to know a memory from every year of your life.
I will plot the curve of your back on graph paper.
I will cut the letters of your name out of each day's
    newspaper.
I want schoolchildren to recite the sequence of your
    DNA.

A GOOGLE MAPS TOUR OF THE HEART

August
Grain Moon

ON A TRAIN TRAVELLING SOUTH, on the east-coast main line, I carry worlds in my backpack. In the newspaper I bought at the station, the prime minister promises new powers to tackle terror threats; marsh warblers and turtle doves are added to the list of endangered birds. I have three books with me, each an invitation into different places and ideas – 1930s Norfolk, the study of fluid dynamics, the blank page – and many more books on my phone. I am dizzy with the competition for my attention over the five-hour journey, astounded by the possibilities available from my train seat. I can tune in and out of conversations in my carriage: four retirees on a day trip to York, two twenty-somethings talking about a mutual friend, the man next to me watching YouTube cartoons with headphones on.

Meanwhile, England passes by at 90 m.p.h.: its hedge-rows and warehouses, its caravan parks and solar farms, flyovers and underpasses. I see a man standing next to a dead beast. I see a kestrel on a post. It's the end of summer and the sun is getting brighter as we head souther.

And then, in my hand, I hold my phone containing the whole internet: all of my friends, the entirety of Wikipedia. The internet is always offering an elsewhere. I spend my days being distracted, attention pulled from this to that. I'm doing well to get anything done at all. Which world do I choose to enter?

I open Google Earth. From 1,100 kilometres out, I have a God's-eye view and spin the globe on the screen with my fingers, like a marble. I have the world between my thumb and forefinger and I pull my territory towards me, like a parachutist coming in to land.

I find Britain, then go north, following motorways and rivers like a migrating bird. I've been living with one foot in the islands and the other in the internet. I have pulled this suitcase up and down the country every few months. This time I'm leaving for a year or more and, as I travel south, my phone finds new networks.

I departed by sea but, inside Google, I approach the islands by air, zooming in: ten kilometres per centimetre, five kilometres per centimetre. I'm reaching down through the sky. My islands are in the palm of my hand: odourless, fixed and digitised, held cloudless in eternal summer. This is where I'm from but the familiar becomes strange.

Pictures taken on rare clear-skied days by commercial satellites or aircraft are stored in huge servers in South Carolina or Iowa or Ireland or Finland and are now called up in an instant and transmitted by fibre-optic cables under oceans and through mobile networks to me, on my train travelling south at high speed.

I hover above the main island. In the satellite pictures, most fields are lush green but in some the grass has been mown or recently reseeded, so I know the pictures were taken just after the first silage cuts in early June. I can tell the time of day by wind turbines like sundials: they cast long shadows to the south-west so it must be early morning.

I move in towards the cliffside farm where I grew up. It is high tide in the picture; some familiar outcrops of rock are not exposed. A stack of silage bales looks, from above, like a black hole. Tracks worn by Dad's tractor are visible across the fields. Sun glints from the roofs of the rusting old vehicles – cars I used to drive – in the field around the caravan.

I look at uninhabited islands, close enough to make out the shapes and shadows of seals hauled out on the rocks. There are digital glitches. Different layers were photographed at different dates and I'm flipping between 2008 and 2010, now 2006, uncovering layers of digital archaeology. I cross a field and I've gone back two years. Always resetting, inside a constantly iterating map, it is all time travel.

Every photograph is of the past. I'm not looking at the island as it is now – with a new season of crops, another year's growth – but at the moment the satellite took the pictures. This is the wave that was captured to stand in place of all future waves.

I zoom in tightly on the steps down to the sea where I had my first kiss. I pan over the turquoise bay where we swam at 2 a.m. one midsummer when it was already getting light. My memories are digitised: draggable, zoomable, pannable. The boy on the beach, face blurred out, fading in my memory. Here we are, above a farm track where I fell to my knees, following roads I drove with my eyes full of tears. With a click I can revisit all the text messages and re-read emails.

A text message brings me out of the maps and back to the train. B says she'll meet me at King's Cross. I zoom out again – there is more world than just the island. The blue dot shows my current location nearing London. I'll soon be among the crowds, warm air and tall buildings, and I begin to pack my books and papers back into my bag.

But, with a flick of my finger, I could be pinging into the Atlantic, as if pushed by an easterly wind, navigating the weather systems of the internet.

Google Maps allows me to access places I never would otherwise, without travel, disturbance, emissions. Google Maps has one billion users. Pictures taken by Google's satellites are used for planning holidays and hovering over memories.

I've stuck paper maps to my walls wherever I've lived, always of somewhere I'm not. In the city, I missed the islands; in my most recent flat, the London streets. Although I like to lay paper maps on the floor, I appreciate more the functions of digital mapping. My mind fizzes and swells with the possibilities of the technology.

The digital maps offer new opportunities to be elsewhere. I sometimes get a feeling I can step into the maps on my screen. Recently, my interest, Streetview-enabled, has returned to cities and I virtually walk the streets of Porto, Prague and Berlin, thinking about where I might go next.

The satellite pictures enter my dreams, making me scroll and search in my unconscious and waking life. In a new city I feel as if I have become the orange Streetview figure, clicked and dropped into strange surroundings.

I'm leaving for another stretch. I don't know quite where I will go. In a London bedroom or a Berlin café or on a different island, distant in a warm sea, everywhere else is closer than ever. I can return instantly at the swipe of a finger. My home will always be there. It is here in my phone and in my heart, the Google Maps icon holding its promise between Facebook and email, fighting for its territory between the Atlantic and the North Sea.

HIGH LONDON

September
Harvest Moon

B MEETS ME WHEN I GET off the train at King's Cross. She has finished work for the day and come to help me with my bags back to her place, another hour east across London by tube and train and on foot. She has a spare room in her flat, usually let via Airbnb, and I can stay for a month, paying rent. We first met through her ex. They split up but we remained friends. She knows the best skips to find fresh food dumped by high-end delis. She knows that getting up early is often worth it.

I've been having an ongoing conversation with whoever is with me. The friend opposite me at the table changes but the thread remains the same. In Andy Warhol's diaries, he refers to himself, Andy, as A, and whoever is with him, a shifting rota of assistants and friends, as B.

B is with me in the art-gallery café, in the passenger seat of my car, standing beside me as I smoke a cigarette outside the swimming pool, walking ahead on a footpath through the woods. I met B when we both wrote for the same magazine, when we lived on the same island, when we posted on the same messageboard and went to certain nightclubs. We meet one-to-one, which I prefer to group situations since I've been sober. We like to eat sushi, go swimming, sit on a bench, go to an AA meeting.

Then there are the digital friends. I have a group message with two girlfriends, a duo of Bs, ongoing for a decade. B pops up in my chat window. B texts. B doesn't reply directly to the question I have asked via email but answers another more obscure question in a comment on a year-old photo. I read B's posts daily but rarely communicate directly.

I've moved job and city and house often and have accumulated Bs with whom I can keep in touch online for ever. We don't have regular contact, so if we meet, it's for an update on everything that has happened in our lives over several months or years.

B told me that in the last week he's spent fifty-five hours playing an online empire-building game. He's been building harbours and skinning deer.

B told me that she's written fifty poems about eggs.

B told me how once, following an impulse, he threw his brand-new digital SLR camera off a bridge into the sea.

B told me about how her family history has made her unable to consider marriage.

And sometimes I forget what I've told you and which city we're in and who you know and how we intersect.

I stand on the balcony of B's twenty-first-floor flat, looking out over London. What I first thought was a shooting star is a cigarette flicked from a balcony above.

I hear traffic, children and swearing below. I see trains passing on a raised track in front of the towers at Canary Wharf. New skyscrapers have been built in the city since B moved in here three years ago: distinctive silhouettes on the western horizon.

The sun is setting behind central London. A screeching herring gull passes, travelling south, then a passenger plane. I look down onto a pigeon, broken aerials and lost balls on the roofs of lower buildings. Lights are turning on as people get home from work.

The building is in need of redecoration but is clean and well ordered. There are notices in the lobby for exercise classes and art exhibitions. The nearby market is cheap, bowls of fruits and vegetables for a pound.

My bedroom looks east. The tower marks the eastern extent of inner London and beyond us are the things that service a city: an Amazon warehouse, gas towers, a lorry park.

I'm thrilled by the planes taking off or coming into land at City Airport. They seem so close up here. I hear them coming and I look them up on my Flight Radar app: they come from Milan or Dublin.

I spend the month trying to make the most of being back in London. I meet old friends, go to poetry readings, join the Climate March along Whitehall shouting for Green Energy Now. I'm looking out for any work or money where I can.

A friend who works at a training hospital appeals for breast models for reconstructive plastic-surgery training and I reply. Standing in a hospital ward, naked from the waist up, breasts marked with felt-tip pen, surrounded by male trainee surgeons, I am suddenly dizzy and faint and have to be helped to sit down, brought a glass of water. What a situation to put myself in for forty quid. Maybe I'm not as tough and liberated as I thought.

Out there, the city is lit up and huge and still noisy with traffic. I'm staying up until the island results comes in.

A week ago, I put my postal vote into a letterbox in Poplar. This afternoon, it was sunny and hot and I went for a bike ride, but I was thinking about home. In the shopping centre under Canary Wharf, my YES badge got some glares. Now, I'm sitting in the dark with the internet on my lap, trying to reconcile my decision to leave Scotland with my desire to have a say in its future.

Mist is coming down over the Shard and Primrose Hill and Tower Hamlets. In the gloom, the flashing light on top of One Canada Square is like a lighthouse. I think about helicopters and boats speeding through the night, carrying ballot boxes from islands and outlying areas up north.

I start to get ready for bed but, just after the island results, voting no to Scottish independence, there is a flash to the west, the beginning of a thunderstorm that will pass over London for the next couple of hours. It is loud and wakes people all across the city, forcing us to stay up for the referendum results.

At 3 a.m., I have a sudden flurry of messages on the dating website I joined a few days earlier. All of us, awakened by the storm and the politics, sit up in bed and, with sudden perspective, realise we're lonely. We reach for our phones, reach out for each other.

As it becomes clearer that the national result is going to be no, the storm rages. It passes easterly over the tower. I stand out on the balcony watching, in sudden heavy rain, feeling like a powerful conductor of the city.

I try to sleep. The wind rattles in the tower's rubbish chutes. Above me, five more layers of people. Below me, twenty more floors, and below that the earth riddled with basements, subways and train tunnels. The number of Wi-Fi networks scrolls off the screen.

On 1 October, I will take a one-way flight to Berlin. I have to go, motivated by loneliness. I think the most important part of the story must be coming next.

HOODED CROWS

October
Hunter's Moon

W HEN I ARRIVE AT SCHÖNEFELD Airport, there are gangs of hooded crows hustling around the runway. They are a common bird on the island but I haven't seen them elsewhere in the UK. They were on the harbour town rooftops, and now they're here in Berlin to meet me. The hooded crows make me feel at home.

In Scotland we call them 'hoodies'. In German, their name is 'mist crow', *Nebelkrähe*. In London, the crows are all black: they are carrion crows (*Corvus corone*), found in England and the south of Scotland. But in other places, with colder winters and higher latitudes, the north of Scotland, Scandinavia, central and eastern Europe, the crows wear waistcoats of grey: these are hooded crows (*Corvus cornix*). Both call with similar 'kraa kraas', but the hoodies are more often found in flocks. Berlin and my island are both just within the hooded crow's range, which opens into the wilder, more sparsely populated regions of Norway and Poland beyond.

The ranges of the carrion crows and hooded crows overlap in what are known as 'hybrid zones', where both species are present. The hybrid zones are moving slowly north-west, and this is a marker of climate change. As temperatures increase, many species of bird and insect are tending to move towards the poles and up slopes.

I am attracted to the northern places that are 'hoodie territory'. The areas pushed ever northwards and constrained as the climate warms are the places I want to visit.

I continue to see hoodies all over Berlin. Crows are generally unpopular birds but must be admired for their tenacity and intelligence. Crows know what is going on in their territory and their behaviour often alerts me to other things, like the presence of birds of prey. If the crows are making a commotion, I know that a buzzard, kestrel or even a goshawk could be nearby.

Birdwatching is the ideal antidote to screen fatigue. Our eyes grow weary looking at closely held phones and computers. Our long-distance vision is underused and blurry. Spending time scanning a distant horizon or treeline gives my eyes a change and, after a while, I feel my vision clarifying. Objects become clearer. I'm coming to my senses, sharpening my eyes.

BERLIN FOR BEGINNERS

November
Hunter's Moon

THERE'S ALWAYS A SENSE OF arriving in Berlin just a little too late. Five years ago, people say, that's when it was really happening. I'd visited once for a weekend, a decade ago. We'd ridden bikes and stayed up all night with friends-of-friends in their large, airy apartment, which they could afford to rent even though they worked only part-time, selling ice cream.

I wanted to come back to a city because I'm not done yet. I want another throw of the dice. People back home seem so sure our little island is the best place to live, when they haven't tried anywhere else. I'm also here because a good way to get over a hopeless crush is to move to another country, where there are new people to get hopeless crushes on.

I didn't choose Berlin for a particular reason: no job, no study, no lover. I'm just here for a change. I know one person here, an acquaintance from London I once had a seizure with, and he encouraged me to come. I booked a one-way flight and a temporary place to stay. I appealed online for friends, asking on Twitter for any Berlin contacts, people I could follow, ask for advice or meet up with. I signed up to Duolingo.

You are free to invent your identity in a new city. I want to act like I'm still in my twenties, maybe get a nose-piercing and an undercut, start being polyamorous, making sculptures. I'm attracted to what I think of as Berlin style: *Cabaret*-via-Cold War, bicycles, minimal techno, black clothes.

I have enough money to survive for a couple of months before I have to get a job, a freeing position I've never been in before. But I have to be careful and live cheaply. If you are poor, Berlin is a better place than most to be. I have scruffy clothes because I'm a broke artist, not because I'm trying to look like one.

I slice off my thumbprint with a bread knife. I get a German phone number.

On my first night in town, I eat alone in a Turkish restaurant, watch attractive men walking past and think I've made the right decision. I calculate that my opportunities for romance here will be better than on the island.

On my first day exploring the city, I try to order in German in a café and they answer in English. I seldom try again. I've had German described to me as both easy and difficult to learn. People have told me it's cheap to live here, then complained that rent is too expensive. Berliners, I'm told, are relaxed and stern, both open-minded and aloof. I'm unsure where I stand.

I do know that Berlin has a high water table, an abnormal aquatic altitude. The city is built on sinking, shifting ground and rising groundwater. I walk to look at a lump of concrete: the *Schwerbelastungskörper*, the 'heavy loading body', a huge 12-tonne concrete cylinder built in 1941 by Hitler's regime to test the site by seeing how much of it would sink into Berlin's swampy, unstable ground.

For the first month I rent a room in an apartment in Neukölln in the south-east of the city, one of the most multicultural, and poorest, areas of Berlin. The room has a loft bed: I'm sleeping close to the ceiling. The landlord lives here too. He's always there, in a side room filled with plants.

In the early weeks, I don't have a routine or friends. I try to fill my days meaningfully and wonder if I've done the right thing by coming here. I'm trying to allow the unexpected, to give space for something magic. I read books about the history of the city. I walk for miles with a strange language around me, investigating new types of corner-shop snacks, watching people. There's a relaxed easy communal atmosphere to everyday life here, at odds with stereotypes of German punctuality, discipline and order. The city is rich in public space – parks, pavements, squares, riversides – where people can linger without being a customer. It's a good place to be underemployed.

Often this freedom – this lack of responsibility – is an asset, this lightness. I can keep myself well, be selfish and spontaneous. But, oh, so often I worry that the loneliness has grown overripe when my day has been long and my lips taste like glue and I've been silent and am not sure I exist at all, and I'm looking for something or someone to weigh me down.

We are far from the sea: bikes don't rust here. I am queasy and dumb.

I start to meet strangers I've been put in touch with by mutual friends.

B, a Brit, is studying for a master's, taking advantage of Germany's lack of tuition fees. She works part-time, like a number of her friends, on a helpline tracking down lost food takeaway orders. She is a pizza detective.

B, an American, has got a job as a nanny and is learning German from the young children.

B lives in a large Marxist houseshare where each week they have a plenum to discuss bread and cleaning.

B moved here to be a DJ but has recently spent less time at clubs and more training to be a life coach.

I call B when I'm near a café he mentioned. He's not there but is friendly and suggests meeting up another day soon. When I hang up the phone, I surprise myself by crying. I acted casual but it means a lot to me. Asking for new friendship is hard. Hearts and futures can turn on a single afternoon or an accepted invitation – but more often lead to nothing but themselves. My stomach churns. I am so open and my hope has remained airborne for so long but I don't know how much longer I can manage.

I find a good falafel place, where I can watch the orange sun setting down Oranienstrasse. Sitting outside, I feel the winter that will soon be closing in. At the end of the road, over the crossing, a mosque is busy. The U1 train passes and blows the ash from the ashtrays. I watch the punks under the bridge.

A strange woman walks past. I've seen her a few times now. She has rolls of fabric fastened around her body. She is upholstered.

I check my space updates. Today a NASA spacecraft reached Pluto for the first time, after a nine-year journey. It has travelled five billion miles from Earth. The flyby, transmitting photographs and information, could see Pluto restored to planet status. It calms me to read the names of Pluto's moons: Charon, Styx, Nix, Kerberos and Hydra. Our solar system keeps operating, celestial dynamics at huge scales of time and distance, keeping us all safely in place.

I go for long walks, across Neukölln, Kreuzberg, Mitte, in a skirt made of cobwebs and a bag of red suede. Every ninth conversation I overhear is in English.

I come to a nightclub, open, strangely, in the afternoon. I walk in, no one stops me, and briefly dance alone under the disco ball.

I register at my local town hall to become an official resident and get the accompanying certificate that will allow me to work. When I tell them I'm British, from the EU, it is no trouble at all.

I go to English-speaking AA meetings full of travelling American business people. Some of their 'rock bottoms' sound no more severe than the average night out in a UK town. I thought this was where I might make friends but I find some of the people odd. They attend five meetings a week and talk about certain visiting speakers as if they are pop stars.

Although I have only seen them once, I often dream of whales.

I receive an invitation to a concert at the music school. I arrive late and sit on the stairs, not really hearing or connecting with the music, and leave early. No one had known I was there. I often feel like that in this city: disconnected, superfluous, weightless.

On the way home I share my U-Bahn carriages with a man wearing a raccoon-fur hat, a Berghain fashion Goth with cropped blond hair, a young couple on phones, a woman in a headscarf asking for money, American tourists, a beautiful girl with a nose ring reading the Marquis de Sade.

Back in the loft bed, I watch easy TV, trying to forget myself. I have a growing feeling that the landlord resents me, or he resents having to let his spare room. He told me he was a personal trainer yet I have never seen him go to work. I can tell he thinks I'm feckless and rich, and in many ways he would be right. The bathroom has no lock. I know he's been coming into my room when I'm out.

One day I go for a swim and, when I lock the heavy

door of the changing room behind me, I immediately relax and realise how insecure I've been feeling. I'm glad I'm leaving the flat soon – my month is up. I go to look at a new place in a street with the same name on the wrong side of the city – the old West rather than the old East.

I've been watching a webcam of a volcano in New Zealand. I've been emailing a man who's cycling across China. What's the weather in your time zone? Tell me about the weather systems of the internet.

Via Craigslist I find a small flat to sublet where I can live alone for November. The artist who usually rents the place is going to the USA for a residency. It's a tiny one-bedroom place, feminine and beautifully decorated, with a dressing screen, a collection of precious stones, a three-quarter bath. The artist has left most of her belongings and it's like I'm play-acting as her for a month. I feel large and clumsy but happy to be here.

An older woman lives alone upstairs. She knocks on the door and asks to use the washing-machine, then brings down a huge pile of clothing, stuffing the machine full. Apart from the laundry, I think she just wants the company. Her English is broken and I think she's telling me the sad story of her life until I realise she's reciting the lyrics of 'Tragedy' by the Bee Gees. She is an old Kreuzberger of a now-rare type, who has lived through many changes in the area. She's maybe in her sixties, wearing headscarves and skirts from another era. I'm a bit scared to open up to her, worried about letting her in because I don't know how long she'll stay.

Late at night, I sometimes see her outside the *Späti* with men a third of her age and a bottle of beer, three sheets to the wind. She has the otherworldly air and the acidic scent of the habitual drunk. Maybe what unnerved me is that she is the ghost of another future.

'At the moment,' I always say. 'I'm living in Berlin *at the moment*,' or *'for the time being'*. Everything is temporary, easy access, instant.

Did I fall asleep or did I just go offline? I texted you in my dream. Sometimes I feel as if I can cut and paste through my body. I want to copy this city's smell of sausages and pollen and send it to you. I'm trying to type and, when you reply, I can feel your finger on the touchscreen.

DIGITAL NOMADS AND GHOSTS

December
Cold Moon

L AST SUMMER, I SAW A digital ghost. I was walking around a Neolithic stone circle on the island, in the early hours, at the first light of dawn. I lifted my phone to take a photograph of the standing stones silhouetted against the sunrise and, on the camera screen, a dark figure was moving across the heather at the centre of the circle. But when I lifted my eyes from the phone, the figure was not there. It seemed to have existed only digitally, on the screen of my internet-enabled device.

The German term *Wanderjahr* (journeyman year) refers to the tradition of setting out to travel after completing

41

an apprenticeship as a craftsman. This year, I'm embarking on a nomadic period, my plan to move around, living in different places, working for remote employers, using communication technology, not tied to one workplace.

I've moved often for years. My Amazon account shows more than twenty addresses — homes and workplaces — where I have had parcels delivered in the last decade. Yet I have kept the same email address. In many ways, the internet is my most stable home.

I am sleeping in a stranger's bed, surrounded by her books and pictures, using her cooking oil and Wi-Fi. When I go, I'll clean the flat and buy new toilet paper and not leave a trace. This is the sublet life. Every month we shuffle. There are layers of subletting, renting from someone who's renting from someone else, with different levels of formality, and so on. Renters keep moving somewhere new but leaving open the option of returning.

The idea, the dream, is that the 'digital nomad' can sell their possessions — or put them into storage facilities or parents' attics, to be reclaimed for the endlessly delayed 'settling down' — and move freely with the seasons. All your books and music and photographs are stored digitally. Unencumbered by a mortgage or children, I exploit cheap air travel and the freedom to move and work within the EU.

Here in Berlin, there are forty thousand English-speaking immigrants, or 'expats', as they often call themselves. Americans and Canadians are able to live in Germany on 'freelance' or 'artist' visas. It's the capital city but not the financial centre (that's Frankfurt), so it's without the banking districts of cities like London or Paris smartening the atmosphere and finance workers pushing up property prices. The empty buildings and cheap rents of the city that make it appealing to me were created, in complex waves of habitation and abandonment, by its brutal history of dereliction and division.

I meet a lot of Irish people here. I also meet Turks and Iranians. My favourite place to eat is the Sudanese sandwich place, where they serve cheap falafel with delicious peanut sauce.

The 'digital nomad' lifestyle is usually more complicated than the fantasy of the laptop on the beach and total integration of work and leisure. It's more practical: to rent a flat in Berlin costs about a third of one in London – pounds paid by UK employers will go further here, and it's less glamorous: I've been broke, under-employed, panic-searching for income. I've met international visitors in this city who can't afford to go home, people who realise they'll never afford to buy a house so decide to keep moving, people never able to find stable work. I've stayed on friends' sofas between sublets and I've faced the bureaucratic problems that come from having no fixed address.

This lifestyle has no safety net of sick pay, pension or stability. It's for able young people who can fall back on family if things go wrong. In the event that I become ill or things get too hard, I will easyJet home.

I'm writing this in one browser tab; the others are open with email, Facebook, Twitter, articles I've started reading, a video I've quarter-watched. I flick open another tab with BBC News. The borders of Europe – at Calais and the northern coasts of the Mediterranean – are busy with refugees trying to enter the countries I freely move between. It's clear what a privilege I have, the luck of the passport I hold allowing a lifestyle some will risk their lives for a chance at.

I click onto Facebook. People are talking about electing a new Labour Party leader, and the Northern Lights that were seen in the skies over the island last night. I look at photos of a baby belonging to someone I was in a pub quiz team with seven years ago, the new profile picture of someone who came to view a room in my flat in 2010, the girlfriend of someone I went on an internet date with, inspirational quotes posted by people I worked with five jobs ago. Social media keeps my links with past lives and locations open. It is brilliant and confusing. I feel omniscient and thinly spread, my mind technologically enhanced yet fractured. I don't know whether to spend my time connecting with old friends online or meeting new people in my city.

B told me that her husband had just received text messages she sent two years ago. Where had they been all that time?

There is growth of this 'sublet' or 'freelance' culture: people always keeping their options open, skimming the surface of other countries, digitally fragmented, never committing. There's an alternative society on Craigslist and Airbnb, cheap-flights websites and Tripadvisor: the people at the gym and the swimming pool in daytime or in coffee shops on laptops, working from wherever, or not working at all. Move between the cool districts of international cities – London, Reykjavik, Melbourne, Berlin – and the currency and time zone change but the people are the same. The only language you learn is how to ask for a coffee and the Wi-Fi password. We talk about our computing equipment and behaviour online like our parents talk about their cars. It's how we get places. All I want is Wi-Fi and a locked door.

In many ways, the internet insulates me from the foreignness of a new place. I can glide around the city looking at my phone, guided by Google Maps, streaming

BBC radio, posting pictures to social media, looking up phrases. Germany barely touches me. But when my phone runs out of battery, I'm lost, unable to read the language or locate myself.

You can travel the world with headphones on, scrolling Twitter. Everywhere in Instagram squares, everywhere on Facebook feeds. Everywhere is the same. Everywhere is me on my laptop sitting up in bed, screenlight pouring into my pupils and keeping me awake. Queuing in the supermarket looking at my phone, in smoking areas and AA meetings and airports in different countries, I could be anywhere or nowhere.

I drop a packet of Rizla from a high window and the papers flutter down into the courtyard like snow.

The same technology that allows my lifestyle – the flexibility, the short-term, the instant – also enables me to be detached and uncommitted. I can exist ordering packages from behind a closed door and with a few clicks can move on. I'm constantly tantalised, through advertisements and the endless scroll, with choices I could have made, haunted by distraction. Everywhere I leave 'data shadows': traces of information left behind as I go about my online life, sending emails, clicking links, paying for things.

I've found lately that when people message me, perhaps suggesting meeting up, or in a potentially romantic situation, they drop personal pronouns – it's all 'Be in touch?' or 'Wanna meet up?' rather than 'Would *you* like to meet up with *me*?' – never implicating themselves, or making firm plans, always suggesting they have somewhere else or better to be. We like to give the impression that things don't mean that much and we're not taking risks.

In my first weeks in a new city, I'm sometimes excited because no one knows where I am . . . and then I feel lost because no one knows where I am. I veer between ebullient and tearful. One day, I block out Berlin with a map of the island stuck to the window and I trace islands and coastlines, absorbed in intricate shorelines. On the U-Bahn or in Lidl I'm sometimes suddenly sad: I left the island because I was lonely, but maybe things will be just the same here.

But then I talk on Skype to my toddler niece back in the UK, via the mobile networks, via fibre-optic cables, passing information held in servers, through data centres and phone lines. It's wonderful: the physical infrastructure of the internet that allows me to connect with those I love from far away. Powerful lasers in steel boxes in unmarked buildings produce the light that travels along fibre-optic cables. In the simplest terms, the internet is made from pulses of light.

I'm about as old as a millennial can be. I didn't have an email address until I went to university at the very end of the twentieth century, but as soon as I got online, I was thrilled and hooked. It was a turbocharged version of the postal fanzine network I'd linked into as a teenager on the island. I soon became a keen user of email, then various messageboards, then blogging site LiveJournal and proto-Facebooks Friendster and Myspace. I went between these sites checking for updates for most of the day at my office jobs. Then, in 2008, I found the internet inside my phone. I've been extremely online for fifteen years, longer than my schooling. The fourth dimension of the internet is part of my consciousness and many of my dreams are entirely digital.

I have a recurring dream of being in a tower block, swaying.

I'm walking to meet a friend in Kreuzberg, and Beyoncé is buffering on my phone, through my headphones, and snatches of the song − lyrics about waking up in the kitchen – come into my ears between the dealers around Görlitzer Park offering me drugs. The digital and the street intertwine. I drove from Scotland to London and went to bed dreaming of satnav. I fell asleep outdoors in an east German forest in dappled sunlight and dreamed about the internet. With my laptop blinking beside my bed, I dream of shooting stars.

I think about my digital ghost at the stone circle, existing only in pixels, condemned always to be online. Was it a glitch or a trick of the light? There is a history of using technology to contact the spirit world. The standing stones, and the methods used to transport and erect them, were the most developed form of 'technology' available to the Neolithic people. For five thousand years, this site has been an important place at the heart of the island, and we'd be misguided to think it no longer works.

We digital nomads are insubstantial, flitting, often pale and nocturnal, living more online than not. It strikes me that my phone is a reflective surface, a mirror. Maybe the digital ghost was simply my own reflection.

BIRDS OF PREY

January
Wolf Moon

I N A CITY FAMOUS FOR its nightlife, I've been waking up early to look for birds of prey. On a Sunday morning, while the techno clubs are still running, I've had a full night's sleep and am out on my bike with my binoculars. I pass people on the street coming home from parties or from working the night shift: getting out of taxis, off the U-Bahn. A pair of wide-eyed girls in boiler-suits with filthy hands are walking arm-in-arm. I cycle past snatches of music and voices from house parties.

It has been cold overnight and, at Tempelhofer Feld, the big park on the site of the old airport, the grass is coated with frost. The rising sun glints in the windows of the airport terminal building – one of the largest structures in

Europe – and the sky is the same pink as the markings on the runway, while everything else is monochrome. Cold is in my nostrils and I can hear trains, traffic and the hooded crows. My fingers hurt when I take off my gloves to use my phone camera. My phone buzzes with messages from the dating site, from men who have not slept, but they are not what I'm looking for now.

A strange thing has been happening lately with my email. I changed my Microsoft location setting to 'Germany' and now hotmail handily translates my emails into English, even if they are already in English. It's my own language but filtered through *Deutsch* and back again. The algorithm thinks it knows best. This is also what is happening inside my mind. I start seeing my Britishness through the eyes of the Germans I meet, and I talk more correctly, how the Germans expect and hope a native English speaker should sound.

People start talking German to me, in the post office, toyshop, U-Bahn, and I feel dumb and under stress because I don't understand. I enrol on an intensive beginners' course, attending every morning for three hours with homework each night. The others in my group at the friendly language school are three Americans, two Brits, an Australian, a Ghanaian and an Israeli. After months of mainly solitude, it feels healthy and good to be sitting around a table with other people on a regular basis. I'm gaining some new words, grammar and tenses but also some structure to my time in Berlin. I learn the German for the punctuation mark we call a 'dash': *der Gedankenstrich* means 'thought pause'.

B told me that when she moved here eight years ago it was more necessary to speak German. Now, it seems English is increasingly prevalent. I see it online, where my German friends often post in English on social media, to be understood by a wider audience, increasing their potential followers.

It's a ten-minute walk from my apartment to the language school across Neukölln each morning. I stop at an old-fashioned bakery for a coffee and to do my day's homework. It's a pleasant daily routine I've created. I could have gone anywhere but here I am learning these few street corners, this language, trying to tether myself. I consider moving on, somewhere warmer, somewhere else. Can I make a life here with this churning in my chest, a pull elsewhere, feeling lighter than I should? These marvellous days are made of learning and change, feeling the ground shift. In six weeks I've made friends and been lonely and had new ideas.

B says Berlin is a confrontational city and that's why she likes it. She also says that it's very slow-moving yet changes very fast, that people here are jaded and enthusiastic. I can't get a handle and meaning shifts. B says this city bombarded the senses but I find the opposite, feeling like I'm in a bubble of non-comprehension, the streets mild and eerily windless.

My old friend B, who is knowledgeable, tells me that dusk and dawn are the best times to see hawks. 'Try to break up your own outline by standing against a tree,' he advises. I've been in the park for just a few minutes when a big bird of prey comes screeching out of the trees, upsetting the hooded crows and changing the atmosphere so the air is charged with alertness. I go, 'Oh, wow,' out loud. It perches on a post – I fumble with my binoculars trying to get a closer look – then flies back into the trees and disappears. I'm a novice birdwatcher so am not sure what species it is but when I get home I compare the call to a recording online. Yes, it was what I was hoping to see: a goshawk.

I'm not quite sure why I came to Berlin but I'm looking for new experiences and inspiration and love. I'm looking for patterns. I came for people, not birds, but I heard that, amazingly, around a hundred pairs of goshawks (*der Habicht* or *der Hühnerhabicht* in German, the 'chickenhawk' rather than the English 'goosehawk') breed and live in the city of Berlin. The northern goshawk

(*Accipiter gentilis*) is, in most places, notoriously elusive, only glimpsed in woodland. In Britain, goshawks were extinct by the late nineteenth century, persecuted by humans who saw them as vermin. From the 1970s, they were reintroduced by falconers and, these birds breeding with others that had escaped from captivity, there are now around 450 pairs in the UK.

I am excited that here in Berlin it is not so hard to spot them, even for a beginner like me. If you have an idea of what to look or listen for, you can, I've heard, watch them from an open-air café or even a swimming pool. In the last thirty years, they have thrived in Berlin where there is an abundance of prey. They hunt and eat mainly pigeons but also other birds, like crows and magpies, and mammals, including rats and squirrels — and they are not usually persecuted by humans.

Goshawks are arboreal, they live in trees, and Berlin is one of Europe's most wooded cities, with tree-lined streets, an average eighty per kilometre, and parks and cemeteries where the trees have regrown after the Second World War, when starving Berliners cut them down for firewood. Although goshawks are found in a few other cities, Berlin has the highest density of goshawk territories anywhere in the world, urban or rural.

In my first days in the city, I found some old yet

functional binoculars from Mauerpark flea market. They have been my biggest expenditure so far in Berlin, apart from rent and the taxi from the airport. I'm happy but often lost and, sometimes, with a lurch, homesick. I've been walking a lot, drifting around this strange city alone, guided by the maps on my phone. The binoculars are a perfect purchase that will allow me to take flight. The things I am looking for are elusive, distant and pass quickly, so I need to be ready.

When you've had sadness, it will cast a shadow long after things are better. The darkness flickers around the edges, threatening, but also providing a contrast.

Goshawks tend to spend much of their time perched, rather than soaring like buzzards, so they can be difficult to find. One useful indicator that a goshawk is perched somewhere nearby is crows and gulls obviously mobbing something in a tree. B told me to look for a very large bird with broad wings and a long tail, and described their distinctive heavy chest and how, when pursuing prey, they tend to fly fast and low.

I start going out looking for the hawks in November at Tempelhofer Feld. It is a wide open expanse ringed by trees, train tracks, apartment blocks and the huge terminal building. The Feld, or field, was a site of early aviation experiments. In the 1920s, the first airport was built in the area. The current building was constructed by the Nazis, designed as part of the Germania project to create a new world capital. It is vast, curving, symmetrical and, when constructed, it was the largest building in the world. There are 400 air raid and gas attack shelters underground.

After the war, Tempelhof was the site of the Berlin Airlift in 1948 and 1949, when West Berlin was supplied by plane. After the end of the Cold War and after German reunification, it was used as the city's main civil airport. In 2008, the last flight took off from Tempelhof. There were plans to develop the site but a referendum decided there would be no construction in the park for ten years. It is now left open to the public, and to wildlife. The planes left and the birds returned. Fast wings still descend over the runway.

I buy a bike from eBay for seventy euros, picking it up from a modern tower block near Treptower Park. B says I'm brave to start cycling in Berlin at this time of year but I know it's the right decision when I get on and, for the first time in years, feel the thrill of the city opening up. My fingers tingle in the cold air, I use muscles in my thighs I had forgotten, head full of all the new German vocabulary and my plans for the evening and weekend, all balanced precariously as I cycle alongside the dark canal.

Each day I cycle across where the Berlin Wall ran, marked by a double row of cobblestones, five times: west then east then west then east then west again. Gradually, I'm able to understand more snippets of German conversation and am becoming familiar with the smell of the snack stand and the florist as I pass. East Berlin is dimmer than Western European cities due to the gas, not electric, streetlights still on this side of the city. On satellite pictures of the city taken at night, the difference between east and west is clearly visible: the west a bright yellow; the east a warmer orange.

My new friend B and I form a Hawkwatch Bike gang. We go to Tempelhof at sunrise on the winter solstice and we see no hawks. We go at sunset on 28 December, when snow is lying. We smoke roll-ups with cold fingers at the top of one of the elaborate viewing platforms – spiral staircases to nowhere – and talk about our prospects in work and love. We scan the trees as we chat and B, who has sharp eyes, spots a goshawk on a branch. I get it in my binoculars. And then there are two, flying:

fast and chunky. They are unbothered by the dog-walkers and skateboarders and runners but harassed by a kestrel and the ever-present hooded crows.

Enthused and encouraged by a couple of goshawk sightings, I do more research. I contact Berlin ornithologist Dr Norbert Kenntner. For the last ten years, in April and May, he has climbed trees where goshawks nest and ringed the chicks. Two and a half thousand goshawk chicks have been ringed in Berlin since the early eighties. One sunny Sunday, Norbert kindly takes me around goshawk territories, mainly cemeteries in Neukölln and Kreuzberg. He plays surf guitar in his car between sites and talks knowledgeably and enthusiastically. He tells me how the hawk uses its long, strong legs and talons to kill its prey. It can kill a pigeon in mid-air. He shows me how to find their plucking posts: piles of pigeon feathers on the ground. He tells me about flagging, when, around mating season, males show their white under-tail feathers.

We see big dark goshawk nests high in trees, and we look to see if they contain any new build: green leaves that show they've been worked on this year. On the top of a steeple in Kreuzberg we see the same male goshawk that is pictured on the Wikipedia entry for the bird. Nearby, in the cemetery, his mate is perched on the nest. I look through binoculars at her, then watch her fly, getting a good view of her pale flecked underside. Later, we see a raven perch on a goshawk nest, which Norbert says is highly unusual. We see their droppings and hear their calls. Crows became agitated. Pigeons disperse.

Armed with knowledge from Norbert, I keep searching, setting my alarm and going out. I dress in layers and wellies like I did back home. I see goshawks maybe half of the times I go to Tempelhof and kestrels every time.

When I see a goshawk I feel thrilled and vindicated. I came looking for something and I found it.

The busiest area of the park for humans – near the allotments, barbecue area, *Grillplatz* and dog run – also seems to be the busiest for raptors. They are not perturbed. A kestrel comes overhead, then perches atop a wooden sculpture. The hawks are often accompanied by a motorcade of crows.

I've been in Berlin for a few months now. As I walk around my new city, on my way to job interviews or first dates, scrutinised and hopeful, I am looking up. I'm thinking about the city like a hawk: looking up at treetops, window ledges and chimneys. Goshawks live in trees but use buildings as hunting perches. I'm looking up at the crosses on top of churches and the crescent moons on top of mosques, at satellite dishes, at the angels and cranes.

I sometimes go, at dusk, to a square near my flat in Kreuzberg where Norbert told me there was a nesting site, to look for hawks but I don't find them: the trees are bare and empty. But then, one midday I am walking home from the night before, hair smelling of smoke, mouth tasting of sex, in late-February sun. Crossing the busy square, I unexpectedly hear the yittering call of the goshawk directly above. I'm suddenly alert. I look up and see a goshawk and a crow in chase. Then they are together in combat for a noisy moment before disappearing behind the buildings. It's an exciting and violent spectacle above my head yet no one else browsing the market stalls or sitting outside a café notices.

A few minutes later, the hawk returns to the square alone, then perches on the church tower. I watch it with my head tilted back, shielding my eyes from the sun, following its high path above the traffic. I'm buzzing. I'm pleased I could identify the call among the other high pitches of Kreuzberg: sirens, babies crying, screeching brakes.

I've become tuned into another frequency vibrating alongside our urban lives. Knowing about the raptors gives another dimension to the city.

The seconds when I see the hawks are brief but, writing in my diary at nights, I realise that the birds are often the best thing in my day. This is my time when job search, money worries and loneliness fall away. A swift sighting of the things I've set out to find gives me hope and leaves me on a high. Their silhouettes burn into my memory. I learn the birding term 'jizz' (from the aviation acronym GISS, or General Impression of Size and Shape) means a quick impression at distance or speed, used to identify birds. At home, I look on internet guides and each time I get better at identification and grow in confidence.

I drink a coffee sitting outside a café while a homeless man with a handsome face talks to me knowledgeably about global economics and the price of avocados. I go to a yoga class in a Brutalist church turned art gallery. The teacher tells us we hold guilt and self-criticism just below our navels and I look down quizzically. I practise headstands. I'm learning to fall well.

Urban birds provide chances for observation impossible in rural areas. Ornithologists are still learning about the species and seeing new behaviour in cities. Goshawks have been seen in Berlin since the mid-seventies but the population boomed in the last fifteen years. It is now levelling out. The city is almost at hawk capacity. The urban birds are vulnerable to disease, and death by flying into windows. In rural areas they can face illegal persecution.

I like knowing that the city is not completely human. Nature is not separate and distant. Wild beasts live among us, unreliant, adaptive, among the train tracks and cemeteries and industrial estates; among domestic dogs and cats, feral pigeons and fireworks. I'm interested in other wild creatures in Berlin: red squirrels, foxes and even feral raccoons. The city is not as tame or discovered as we might think.

The hawks become a mascot of my first months in a new city when I find it hard to know what to hang on to. They are something to pursue when my priorities are unclear.

FERAL CREATURES OF THE INTERNET

February
Hunger Moon

WOLVES ARE RETURNING TO EUROPE. They were hunted almost to extinction in the twentieth century but, in recent years, isolated groups have returned in Italy, Spain, France and Poland. As young wolves leave their packs, populations spread. I heard that they blow into eastern Germany with the cold winds from Siberia, over the Polish border. I imagine them on the outskirts of the city.

B, who is a few years younger than me, says that I should be pleased I'd avoided being weighed down. 'But I want to be weighed down,' I reply. I've been light and wind-tossed for too long. I want to make a decision and stick to it. I'm tired of having my options always open. Bring the weights, I'm ready.

So I'm online, trying to get a German bank account, a tax reference number and a boyfriend. There are a lot of single people in this town: perpetual adolescents, forty-year-old students, scenesters and musicians jaded with London or New York.

Lonely one Saturday night, I realise there is a whole city out there: bedrooms like this with other people who feel like me. I've glanced into them passing on the S-Bahn. They won't know I'm here too unless I let them. I have a moment where I feel in control of my fate. I have registered with a dating site but now I will be bold. I type my requirements into the form: gender, location, age range. This dating site uses algorithms to decide which potential mates to show me, becoming more informed all the time, knowing me better than I know myself.

I send out some messages. I'm upbeat and open and optimistic. I'm struck by the contrast between the light lines I send – 'Hi, I like your profile!' – and their weighty implications: do we, two strangers, want to become each other's most important people? Being on the site is to make yourself vulnerable, to admit desire and dissatisfaction. Brave souls! Looking for love on the internet, any new message could be the one that changes everything.

I begin to call some birds by their German names:

Amsel, Rotmilan, Nachtigall. I listen for the laughing of
the green woodpecker. From my bedroom, I hear magpies
and great tits and sparrows and hooded crows. An animal
subculture is living off the things we discard. As humans
become more urbanised, so do animals. There are
mammals in the city: foxes and feral cats. There are rabbits
and hedgehogs and martens. They live in the drains and
the rooftops and the shadows, the places we don't look.

People seem to have 'projects' here. B's project is to
gather people together to sit in silence on an art-gallery
floor and read their own books. B's project is to swim
in fifty-two of the lakes surrounding Berlin, one every
week for a year. B's project is sex parties. My project is
to find a raccoon and a lover.

Raccoons are not native to Europe yet they have been
living, and thriving, feral here in Berlin for the last fifty
years. There are thousands in the city.

I get more messages on a Friday night. Here we are,
alone and screen-lit, with an empty weekend suddenly
ahead. I've had messages from married men, from men
with fetishes for tall women, people in Kreuzberg and
Minnesota and Istanbul and the Cape Verde Islands. A
stranger sent me naked photos and it wasn't entirely
unwelcome. Sometimes I reply and even arrange meetings.

I walk to our agreed meeting place feeling nervous,

but when I meet my date I realise he is more scared than I am. If I wanted to I could savage him.

In a Thai restaurant, he eagerly tells me of his esoteric interests (Tajikistan, hot yoga). After he says goodbye, I am exhausted from trying to present my whole person and take in the whole of him. I realise I will need more resilience and restraint.

I meet someone who DJs and works in a cool bar and has cool hair and would have appealed to me in my twenties. He tells me he has trouble finishing things. But when he sits next to me, I realise how much I want physical affection. I would have kissed him if he had wanted. My body is so lonely and has been for years.

All I want is a shoulder to lie on.

I've heard different stories about where the raccoons in Berlin come from: either that they are descended from pets kept by American GIs, or from animals that escaped from bombed fur farms. I speak to Derk, a city ranger working for the government, and he tells me the true story: in 1945, in the aftermath of the war, a fur farm in north-east Berlin could not afford to feed its raccoons so decided to free them. South of the city, around the same time, they were released for game. The two groups have mixed together to form the population in Berlin today. Derk's current estimate is that there is a minimum of eight hundred raccoon families in the city.

I ask everyone I meet if they have seen a raccoon. B works in a bar so walks home late at night and has seen them running under cars, near bins B saw one when he was pissing at the end of a garden. B saw one up on a twelfth-floor balcony.

My new friend B puts on an old movie and gives me a duvet. Her kindness in a strange city helps a lot. She tells me about how she was catfished. The person she had been messaging for some time was not, she began to suspect, the same person as in their profile pictures on the dating site.

Meanwhile, B uses Tinder to meet people while lonely on work trips to new cities. B uses Grindr when his boyfriend is out of town. B met her ex on Soulmates, then met her husband through him.

After meeting in the bar on my street, I spend the night with someone I've just met. Even though I can tell he is distracted – his mind on someone else – it's so good to sleep next to someone again and I'm not bothered if it doesn't go further. I walk home across Kreuzberg looking for hawks, feeling more human, softer and rounded.

★   ★   ★

After the sublet at the artist's place, I move to a more relaxed apartment in Kreuzberg, with stinging nettles around the door, sharing with the brother of an ex-boyfriend from the UK. My flatmate works in a call centre and makes dubstep. The bath is next to the window; I watch the moon. I think I'll stay here for a while.

One night at 2 a.m., just after I've moved into the flat, I am woken up by a noise, an animal noise somewhere between a cat and a baby, and I think immediately, 'That's a raccoon,' as the yittering mixes with my dreams.

And all I want is a bi-daily source of suggestive text messages.

Berlin has a large proportion of green space, about 40 per cent of its area, so it's easy for raccoons to find places to live: on houses and in trees. They are highly intelligent and sensitive animals, especially in the use of their claws. They eat fruit, nuts and grains from trees, in parks and gardens. Raccoons are opportunists. Urban animals often become better at problem-solving than those in the country, learning how to negotiate roads and avoid humans. Studies have shown that finches from urban environments perform better at challenges than their rural counterparts. The complexity of urban life demands adaptability and intelligence.

I am early for a date so I go into a nearby shop where

the assistant is dismantling a mannequin, its torso and arms on the carpet, ready to be reassembled and re-dressed.

I hate the pretence of first dates when you talk about where his first flat in the city was or the mildness of the winter, anything apart from sex or reproduction or love or the bottomless ache that made you sign up to a dating website in the first place and willingly endure the indignity of walking into a bar with a nervous stomach and going to the bathroom and looking in the mirror at your sorry fucking face. What makes you think it'll be any different this time? It ends either in short, sharp disappointment or drawn-out confusing disappointment.

I'm looking for the moment when our eyes meet, that connection with another, with the wild. I might find it if I'm brave and nocturnal, if I push on through the cold dawns and the awkward meals. There are text conversations that suddenly end – ghostings. There are confusions, such as someone who is always online and likes all my photos but never replies to my invitation.

I want to see a raccoon for myself, but to do so I will need to get up early and linger by the bins, or stay out late and go climbing.

★ ★ ★

I decide tonight is the night. I start the raccoon hunt with a literary reading at a jazz bar. Then I set out at my usual bedtime, 11 p.m. or so, which in Berlin is going-out time for partiers. I feel a bit ridiculous and don't know what I'll find. Others I've told seem perplexed by my plan or think it's a joke but although I'm laughing I'm serious. I want to find a raccoon in the city and I intend to stay up all night in the hope of doing so.

A cold wind blows down Skalitzer Strasse, over the cobblestone pavements, through the spring-green trees, clattering bikes, past the *Apothekes*, *Kniepes* and *Spätis*. An old man is shouting on the phone and the only word I catch is 'sugar'.

I've been trying on seven-hundred-euro dresses even though I have no money. I've been taking my empty glass bottles to the exchange machine, then buying a packet of tobacco with the money. I've been sharing on social media anonymous body parts – feet, shoulders – of people I'm on dates with, in photos I've coyly selected. I've been carrying a whale's tooth from the island in my pocket.

Raccoons are nocturnal and particularly active at dusk and dawn, like the hawks. One way to spot them is to listen to the crows, which make a different noise when raccoons are in the area. Raccoons are capable of climbing into crows' nests, eating their eggs and young, so the crows are on high alert. Both species are known for their intelligence.

What are the animals that shriek in the night?

Interacting with German men made me realise how, in conversation, I'm constantly trying to put the other person at ease: making tiny adjustments, laughing at things that aren't funny. They do not do this. On several occasions, it takes a moment to realise that his neutral tone is not critical, simply neutral. It shows me that I can learn to be genuine in my enthusiasm, to save it.

I meet someone whose profile picture I have admired for months, before I even came to Berlin: a handsome man sitting on a Berlin rooftop in a photo that could have been taken any time since the advent of colour photography. Like magic, I find myself sitting with him at a dark table in a Greek restaurant talking about car-hire schemes. At best, online romance can feel like we've utilised technology to make our dreams come true, even if the dream guy turns out to be the sort of person who keeps trainers in boxes without wearing them.

I meet a man from the internet in a cocktail bar. I drink Fritz-Kola and he drinks liquor and tells me about Mexico, national service and scriptwriting. He is vicious about what he calls 'observational poetry'. Literature should seek to change things, he says.

I have noticed that I can't pick up on class signifiers in German: the subtleties of difference in accent due to education or background or area are inaudible to me. I can't decode the fashion: the upturned collars or tucked-in trousers that might mean one thing at home have different connotations here. I go on a date with a political blogger, thinking he must be some kind of posh boy but find he's a working-class real talker, railing against the urban elite. We talk about privacy and anonymity and media bias and Mount Etna.

I meet someone whose photographs must have been ten years old and who hadn't mentioned his children. I feel apologetic as I cut the date short but I know it won't go further.

There are thousands of sexual opportunities out there on the internet in my phone and my city but somehow I'm struggling to find a match. I have five first dates and no second.

Sometimes I miss the indiscretions of alcohol. One night I get home and cry because it hadn't been fun: it had felt like a job interview. But I have realised that casual sex is possible sober. I can still fall into bed with someone. I just do it intentionally now, without regrets.

I wear the same outfit for most of the first dates: skinny trousers, a big T-shirt that falls off my shoulders, a thick chain around my neck and heavy bracelets, like an escaped prisoner. Blood-dark lipstick.

It's impossible to tell Brits from Germans if they're naked. Clothed, there are tell-tale markers – the white trainers that German men like to wear with jeans, the real tough punk look of some Berliner women. But in his bed at 6 a.m., I can't tell.

Maybe my favourite thing about sex is thinking about it the next day on the U-Bahn, remembering how his body had felt as the automatic announcement on the platform tells us to stand back: '*Zurückbleiben, bitte.*'

I want to kiss you in the CERN supercollider.
I want to kiss you in the International Space Station.
I want to kiss you in Yayoi Kusama's Infinity Room.
I want to kiss you during a leap second.
I want to kiss you for eight minutes and twenty seconds,
the time it takes sunlight to reach the earth.

On the raccoon hunt, my heart rate increases as I enter Görlitzer Park. I've heard warnings not to come here at night: there have been muggings and attacks. I tuck my hair into my hat and put my wallet into my inside pocket.

75

Groups of guys hang around here at all times of day and night, selling drugs. It's the place to come in Berlin for weed or spice or whatever.

I approach some dealers and ask them if they've seen any raccoons. They are bored, I figure, and hanging around the park all night, so there might be a chance they've seen some. It takes a while for them to realise what I'm talking about. I end up talking to Malik about the wild animals in his home country of Gambia. He is surprised that people travel there just to see bats.

He's been in Germany for two months. 'Welcome to Europe,' I say weakly, looking at the park bench on this cold night. He says he comes from the countryside. There are a large number of Gambians newly in Germany, often without even refugee status, often selling drugs to pay for the journey they took and to send money home. We talk about tigers and sunshine, and it is an unexpectedly nice conversation in the middle of the night in a dirty park.

I stride on. I feel good alone and going somewhere. I'm feeling more and more like myself. The more I walk the more confident and in-tune I feel: mind and body working together. I need to keep walking. My phone counts 15,000 steps before the battery runs out.

Feral creatures can disrupt ecosystems. Raccoons eat

wild birds' eggs and destroy nests, damage property. Raccoons can survive in many places, country or city. Should they be celebrated or exterminated?

Derk tells me about a remarkable phenomenon: raccoons 'react to being hunted'. When they are being persecuted, more females are born, both in numbers and proportion of the total. On the other hand, when food resources decline, more males are born. The males go to a new area. Therefore, he says, 'it is not possible to control a population', because hunting or starving them will only make more animals be born or the population disperse. This knowledge led to the decision by the authorities not to try to control the population at all, but instead to leave it up to people to secure their own property.

In Derk's twelve years working for the city, it has been very rare for wild animals to attack humans and even these incidents tend to be misreported or are due to human stupidity. 'Most people don't want to kill animals,' he says, 'but they are angry or don't understand. We need to understand how to live with animals.'

I ask a dog-walker in poor German if he'd seen *Waschbär* (German for raccoon) and he thinks I am asking for a bar. I ask the cashiers in McDonald's: I think the staff might see them when putting out the rubbish. He shakes his head while smiling.

The late-night restaurants are closing. A couple are kissing passionately before she cycles away. Another couple are smiling at each other in the window of a bar, the woman posing alluringly.

And all I want is that moment where your pupils expand and your heart floods open.

I'd be lucky to see a raccoon but I need to put myself in the way of luck. I'm trying to think like a raccoon: tenacious, adaptable. They're not owned or controlled by anyone. I'm liberated, far from my parents or anyone who has ever known me, far from my reputation. I've harnessed the internet and I'm on the prowl. My teeth are sharp.

I've been listening to recordings of their call and have tried to master an impression. It's a furious chittering.

I see the police busting a party: all the guests and a band with full equipment, standing angrily on the pavement outside. It's too loud here for raccoons. My resolve is flagging. At 3 a.m. I call off my hunt for the night and walk back to my flat.

★   ★   ★

At some point in my online dating I get cocky, speedy with the power of being young and female and working the algorithm. I know that if I change my profile picture, I'll get more messages. I count in minutes until I get a response to viewing someone's page. It's the gamification of human relationships. I'm shopping for people, reducing them to a series of qualities, zooming in on my possible futures. I'm aware, as a recovering alcoholic, of the dangers of cross-addiction. The buzz of sexual attention combined with internet apps is heady.

I take a step back and try coolly to analyse my desire. Why do I need a man? I can support myself, move and live as I want. Is it biology or patriarchy that has made me put so much of my energy into this search? I decide I just want to connect with the animal in me.

The water is hard in this city. My soap doesn't lather, my kettle fills with limescale and I miss the soft waters of home.

A few days later, I decide to do the other half of the night: by getting up early instead of staying up late. I'm up before dawn and out on my bike, gliding through empty streets with a sick early-morning feel. I am alert for raccoons and goshawks. The streets are clear but there are a few people around: bin men, early workers, returning partiers, rough sleepers. Over an hour, the sky changes from deepest blue to almost white.

I cycle past Alexanderplatz TV tower to Brandenburger Tor and am there with the first tourists of the day. They've all got North Face written on their left tit and screens hanging around their necks.

In Treptower Park, several nightingales are singing loudly from neighbouring bushes. The day has arrived and I haven't seen a raccoon but I've seen disturbed bins and trails in the undergrowth. The raccoons are tantalisingly close but invisible, hiding in the shadows and dark, up high and down below, the dimensions I can't access. They are on the edges of our lives – the edges of our living spaces and waking hours.

In a cafe in Tiergarten, I meet a serious, beautiful young academic who pulls me up for making generalisations about nationalities and holds my eye. The second we leave the café, we both light nervous cigarettes and this makes me like him even more. We walk through the zoo and see antelopes and ostriches. He is gazing ahead and I look at the side of his face and it's nice. When we hug goodbye, I feel his back through his shirt and I keep thinking of it after.

On our second date, in a Kreuzberg back bar where we can smoke, I find out about his travels and studies. He has an unusual intensity and old-fashionedness.

By our third date, it becomes apparent to me that the dynamic between us isn't right. I want to look after him more than sleep with him. I know I probably won't see him again but I feel quite all right about that, as I leave him and get on my bike. As I cycle, I think about how I saw him before he saw me, hopping slightly from foot to foot with nerves, and how I'm learning things about myself and what I want. My phone runs out of battery so with no GPS I get lost on my bike for an hour or two, confused and okay, roads and pavements empty, late-night *Currywurst* stands, my dimly glowing bike lights, a glance up at the light of the TV tower to help with my sense of location. The stars are out and I can see the Pleiades.

These German men I've met from the internet. I've barely thought about them since I walked away, onto the U-Bahn, into my stairwell, out of their beds. They had no links to my own social circles. A few days later I can't recall their names or faces. They fade like a dream.

I'm entering a corner shop in Mitte when I pass, coming out, a man I went to dinner with a few months previously, the guy I thought was too eager to please. He looks through me blankly and I am deflated. This instant-access romance works both ways.

Where do your dreams go when you forget them?

I've not fallen in love but I'm learning a lot. I'm learning about treating people with respect, even when you're rejecting them. I've realised some of the mistakes I'd made in the past. I can see now the power I had over certain people's feelings without knowing it at the time.

The raccoons have become a symbol of this area of plucky, scrappy Kreuzberg. The big 1 May party in the courtyard of our apartment block has raccoon-hand stamps. The raccoons are known for resilience and adaptability that I hope to emulate.

I still don't know if it was a raccoon I heard from my bed that night but I know they are out there on the rooftops, moving silently and unknown above the red tiles and graffiti. I know that we make enough rubbish to feed colonies, to build another city from, to shelter a species.

Wild animals are wary, careful with their trust. These days, I'm always leaving and going home sober and alone.

I don't feel bad as I cycle away from my date, past witches using cash machines and zombies queuing for *Currywurst*. I feel quite all right, content, in a new city, surrounded by a strange language and monsters and ghouls, inventing myself, looking forward to swimming in the morning, remembering how far I've come, among all the Berliners in big scarves and thick jackets. I changed my life even though it was hard and scary. I feel proud. I've come to a new country and made some friends and got work. A small amount of euros comes into my new German bank account each week. I'm learning the language, I'm almost busy, I have a life and a routine where for the first month I was lost. As I arrive back on the street that is beginning to feel like home, the happy realisation is sinking in that – no matter who I meet or don't meet on the dating sites – I have already pulled it off.

CASUAL LABOUR

March
Worm Moon

I AM BROKE AND LET EVERYONE I meet know that I'm looking for work. The economy is slow in this city and it's not easy to find a job as a foreigner. I look, with varying degrees of seriousness, into the possibilities of working in refugee outreach, as a dominatrix, digging graves and returning stranded turtles to the sea on Ascension Island in the South Atlantic.

I hear about the tea place from a friend of a friend: jobs are available working in the warehouse of a company that imports and sells high-end speciality tea. They are taking on new staff to process Christmas orders.

In order to work, I have to leave the language school. My German teacher warns that a few weeks in is a bad time to stop learning a new language but I need to earn money. I resolve to keep up my studies in my own time, but she's right and what I've learned quickly fades from my mind. I rarely speak German again. About half of the people in the tea warehouse are native English speakers and the other half speak it very well.

Our job is to pack the tea by hand into individual bags. We deal with sacks of fragrant tea and flowers: white and jasmine tea from China, Assam and Darjeeling from my India, green tea from Japan, dried roses and lavender and ginger. We weigh it on scales, like drug-dealers, and pack it with our hands in surgical gloves, sometimes wearing dust masks. The tea sells, in a smart store in the middle of the city, for prices high enough to justify paying us the German minimum wage, rather than exporting the jobs to the developing world.

Everyone who works here is, like me, from elsewhere and living in the city to pursue creative ambitions. The others are musicians, painters, photographers and artists. We represent a subculture in Berlin of Western twenty- and thirty-somethings who have chosen not to have regular work, who have chosen uncertainty and are privileged to do so. We are a highly educated bunch of factory workers, international wannabes thinking of other things. Not coming back after the weekend is a victory:

a colleague doesn't turn up and we wonder hopefully if he's sold a painting. We're all waiting for the email that will change our lives.

I find the repetitive work soothing. It is reassuring to have a well defined task with a start and end time. During orderly, productive days, I weigh tea and fold paper bags and stick labels. I listen to podcasts about the sleep patterns of animals, about foghorns and heartbreak, about the political mood of Greece and surrogate mothers in Thailand. I fold hundreds of pieces of brown paper as the day passes, the sky moves from grey to black and my mood changes from anxious to calm to tired. I could have gone anywhere in the world, I think, and here I am spending my days in an industrial estate in suburban Berlin in winter.

While we are weighing and folding and sticking, we talk. I have conversations with my fellow tea-packers about the impossibility of true translation, about methods of international smuggling, about grants for artists, while stapling thousands of tea bags to pieces of card, while weighing 51-gram quantities of tea into crisp brown paper bags.

A Polish artist tells me that in seven years of living in Berlin she hasn't learned German, and thus is defended from news and society and advertising, and can concentrate on her work. A Canadian painter tells me about his studio, cheaply rented from property developers who want to give their newly built apartments a desirable, arty edge.

Every Monday morning, I give them an update on my online-dating situation and they offer advice on my next move: how to tell someone that our third date was our last, what to do about the dude who always flakes out. Our work tables become the most convivial place I've spent time in years. We become friends and meet up outside work.

The warehouse staff represent a cross-section of Europe and the English-speaking world: Serbians and Canadians, British and Spaniards. I pity the Americans with their visa-application processes, appointments with expensive lawyers and piles of paperwork with an uncertain outcome, at the whim of an immigration officer.

Most of the friends I make are other Anglophones. At a party, I notice that one half of the room is talking German, the other English, moving gently apart. Some of my friends, those who perhaps think they will be in the city longer term, make more effort to integrate.

We don't have guaranteed hours but this suits us. We can drop the job as easily as it could drop us. It is casual work. We have casual relationships. It is a casual city.

We are having sexual adventures in the Eurozone. I am a highly privileged immigrant, not so much an economic migrant as a lifestyle migrant, coming here seeking new experiences, like so many who leave the UK for other parts of Europe: retiring to Spain, buying a house in the South of France. It's not a necessity.

In Berlin, where reminders of terrible history are everywhere – the bronze cobblestones, *Stolpersteine*, on every street bear the names of Jewish people taken from the houses – it is easy to see why a peaceful union of nations like the European Union makes sense. Although I come from its very fringe – I grew up on a cliff looking west to the Atlantic – I am a proud European. I tend to tell people I'm Scottish rather than British. I want to be from a small peaceful country, somewhere modern and international.

Smoking on my balcony at 1 a.m., wondering if I will return to the UK, I hear wild geese passing high above. The migrating animals don't know about national borders. I will leave the tea warehouse but retain excellent abilities to fold brown paper and weigh precise amounts. I declare myself a citizen of Scotland and the internet and the sea.

DIVING INTO BERGHAIN

June
Strawberry Moon

YEARS AGO, B TOLD ME that the best way to get through a crowd at a nightclub or concert is to dance your way through. The bodies around you will have more sympathy for a dancer – they'll shift and accommodate, flex and bend – than for someone simply pushing.

I remembered that advice this midsummer, at the techno club, where not only were most other people intoxicated but were also speaking German. I was disoriented but the best way through my discomfort was to dance. On the dancefloor, I had the sensation that we were deep underwater, swimming in bass. The dancers were seabed beasties: crabs and urchins and anemones. I could luxuriate in the strangeness, in the beat, my arms floating up, light and smoke caught in the bubbles.

A lot of my twenties was spent in discos and bars and clubs but the nights got wilder then worse, and I ended up in rehab. I have not been back to a club for four years but, this summer, I planned a field trip. I would make a controlled scientific excursion to a nightclub. On the solstice, I would go, sober and alone, to Berlin's famous Berghain, a huge techno club with 1,500 capacity in a 1950s electrical power plant, built when it was East Berlin, part of the GDR.

For the last three years, I've spent my time in Orkney. I spent my time there relearning the landscape and rebuilding myself: swimming in the sea, watching seabirds, taking boat trips to small islands. I went snorkelling and was amazed by what I saw in cold Scottish waters: exotic colours, brighter below the surface than above, and wonderful creatures, like sea slugs and urchins. I regained some wonder at the world and the sea helped me in my sobriety. Now, I want to apply the things I've learned about observing nature to the city and to people.

Berlin is 600 kilometres from the ocean and often, because the sea has become so important to me, I wonder why I've moved here. In most of my Facebook profile pictures I am on the edge of a cliff or entering water. How can I find these places in Berlin? Unmoored and drifting far from home, I'm seeking the sea in a land-locked city. B sent me some seaweed held in resin so I can carry the ocean around my neck. And I've been finding water where I can: visiting swimming pools, lakes, saunas, and even a flotation tank. But I did not expect to find the sea in a techno club.

It's midsummer's day, the height of the year, and I'm wearing my seaweed necklace as I approach Berghain. It's Sunday evening and the party is still continuing from the night before. I have a notebook and am incognito in black clothes. The building looms above, huge like a container ship, and I'm nervous. Sailors, I'm told, wore one gold earring to pay for their funeral if they were washed up on a strange shore. The club has a notorious and mysterious door policy that sees scores of people turned away every night. The guy in front of me is unlucky, perhaps too drunk: the stern doormen shake their heads, and he walks away, resigned. But they let me past and I text B, *See you on the other side*, before I put my phone away for the night.

The club retains many of its industrial fittings, and as I climb the steel staircase to the main room – the old turbine room with a high ceiling and concrete floor – the noise hits me. The immense volume of the music creates a full-body experience. I can feel it in my eardrums, my stomach and bowels and through the soles of my feet. It makes my chest throb. It's loud enough to swim in.

Entering that place is like entering a huge echoing cliff cave and, once my eyes have adjusted to the dark, finding it full of rock doves and black cormorants, on shadowy ledges, darting past. I've found a complete ecosystem. Five hundred people or more, a bloom of jellyfish, are drifting with the tide of music. Exquisite creatures appear from behind pillars and speaker stacks like rocks: fashion Goths and techno gays, in leather and mesh and Lycra and neoprene and swimsuits, every type of black. They are dancing with fans, topless in chain mail, showing off their tattoos. I am reminded of the exquisite illustrations of Ernst Haeckel, the German naturalist and philosopher who, at the beginning of the twentieth century, made detailed studies of sea life, including technical drawings of jellyfish and anemones, beautiful and weird.

Underwater, sound travels faster and objects look slightly magnified. Due to the refraction of light in water, they appear closer and larger. A similar effect is created in a club due to the smoke machine, the dark and the drugs. It's hard to tell distance, time or direction. I'm swimming in murky water. A white spotlight is like a shaft of sunlight reaching down to the seabed. There are red lasers and green exit lights. I can't tell how long I've been here.

The people who first settled on this riverbank in the seventh century named the area, some say, 'Berl' after a Slavic word for 'swamp'. The city is inland but an average of just 35 metres above sea level. Huge pipes pump groundwater out of construction sites. Buildings battle against sinking and floods. The city has plenty of water, it is just below ground, and in the months I've been here I've been somehow divining it.

This winter in Berlin, I went to a swimming pool with a wave machine and was sloshed around with chlorine and ten-year-old boys. At Marek's Saunahaus, the room was filled with fragrances of eucalyptus, sandalwood and juniper. Afterwards, I rubbed my body with crushed ice. Naked, in the tiled dome-roofed room at Neukölln Stadtbad, I immersed myself in a circular pool with water jetting from the mouth of a marble frog, the temperature of blood. I had stayed in the sauna until my heart beat so fast my body panicked. I went out into the cooler air then, pointing toe first, into the cold plunge pool. Submerged to the neck, pores contracting, my skin tightening and reacting all around me, it was like I was in an island rockpool.

Now it's summer: I've been following rivers and canals out of the city, on S-Bahn lines and cycle paths. Lake swimming is popular here. I keep a list of places I have swum: Müggelsee, Schlachtensee, Grunewaldsee. I swam in a lake I later found out was meant for dogs, the *Hundestrand*. I swam in a pool on a barge floating in the River Spree and in the wonderful public *Sommerbad*s, one in each borough: open-air lidos with both heated and cold pools.

In a *Hinterhaus* off a smart street, I was given complimentary tea and shown to a relaxation area before being led to a pyramid, like a cheap science-fiction film set. This was a flotation tank, otherwise known as a sensory deprivation tank, and was my capsule for an hour. I was left to shower and enter six inches of highly salinated water. It was saltier than the Atlantic, salty enough to hold my body. Unencumbered by clothes or furniture or floors or gravity, I lay back. The water was body temperature so I lost any point of contact, and the only sensation came from my body. I noticed twinges and tension and relaxed them out.

With my ears underwater, I could mainly hear my own breathing and heart but also doors opening and closing in the buildings and, every few minutes, a U-Bahn train rumbling deep below. I turned the lights off and, as the air above the water in the pyramid began to warm, my sense of location became indistinct. For just a moment, I had the sensation that my body was travelling, bullet-like, at great speed through space. I was like a baby in a womb, and when the lights flashed on at the end of my hour, I was ready to be born, naked and dripping in saline.

When I got out, gravity was more of a drag than usual and I realised I was nothing but an addict, seeking drug-like experiences and different ways of altering my state of mind. I'll drop fifty euros on a flotation tank rather than a gram of coke and still feel the salt dripping down the back of my throat. But these bought experiences are often disappointing: simply paying and lying back waiting to be enlightened does not work. I want to confront and enjoy my senses rather than being deprived of them, and to gain the rewards of effort and imagination.

★　★　★

Often, on a Friday or Saturday night in the cottage on the tiny island where I lived alone for two winters, I wanted to be on a crowded dance-floor in small clothes with sweat running down my back. I felt like an old woman before my time, beside the fire with a blanket over my knees, and missed the throb of the city and of nightlife. Lately, I've learned the German word *'Fernweh'* (literally 'distance pain'), which describes the feeling of wanting to be somewhere else, like a reverse homesickness (*'Heimweh'*), a longing for a place that isn't where you are.

Now, I'm back in the nightlife I missed; I'm exhilarated but awkward. Berghain is a cool place and I like it a lot: hard-edged and minimal and tolerant. The door policy seems to keep out the worst leering men. There are no mirrors anywhere in the club. For the first hour or so, I wander around, looking in the different rooms. There are 'dark rooms' on the ground floor where people can meet strangers for sexual encounters. Berghain started life as a gay club and heterosexuals still take second place. I queue at the bar to buy Club-Mate, a fizzy caffeinated drink popular here. I roll cigarettes in the seating areas, watching couples talking. Their mouths are moving but the loud music means I can't hear what they are saying, like underwater communication.

On the way in, the door staff put stickers over the camera on my phone. There is an open-minded attitude here to nudity, drugs and sex, yet taking a photo will get you thrown out. It's highly refreshing that everyone's not filming stuff. It's hard for internet kids, by which I mean it's hard for me, to have an unphotographed experience but I'm really here more than ever. This is not a place for observers but for active participants.

After a while, I know I can't stay smoking where two different DJ sets from the main room and the Panorama Bar jostle together uncomfortably. At some point I have to let go and swim. I realise that, after all these years, I still have the bass in my body. I drain my Mate bottle, take a deep breath and dance my way to the centre.

There is nothing to do but dive in. The dance-floor is the seabed and I am scuba-diving. My heart beats in time with the music, which builds in layers shot through with chimes, like sonar from a submarine or whale song. Earlier in the day, I watched a documentary about marine life and now its images – schools of fish, breaching whales, curling waves – are swimming through my mind and merging with the activity in the club. The film was in French with German subtitles, reflecting the disorientation I feel in this city.

The Bajau people in the south-west Philippines live

an almost completely seaborne life, in small boats and houses on stilts out to sea. Many never set foot on land, apart from to trade, when some experience 'landsickness'. The Bajau have physically adapted to an aquatic life, developing clear underwater vision, negative buoyancy and the ability to hold their breath for long periods.

It's been exactly four and a quarter years since I last drank alcohol, a few months more since I took drugs. I stopped drinking on the spring equinox, shortly before entering a three-month rehab programme, and every equinox and solstice since then marks another quarter-year sober. I like to celebrate these dates. As my body is moved by the brutal music, I think about where I've been on recent solstices − the top of a hill, the stone circle, the Atlantic coast − places my sobriety has enabled me to visit. A nightclub might be a strange place to celebrate a sobriety anniversary but it's been long enough that I know I won't drink and I have unfinished business. I'm looking for a part of myself I left behind. I lost the active addiction but I don't want to lose her, the tall brave girl with long pale arms and flushed cheeks. I'm chasing myself through the crowd on the dance-floor. I catch glimpses of her white shoulders, her vibrating jaw, her trailing handbag. She's always swimming away from me.

I take a break from dancing, and on a metal staircase up the side of the building, I watch the light fade on the first half of the year. The sky is pink behind the wholesale warehouses of Friedrichshain, behind a Mercedes sign and passing aeroplanes. I think about the tilt of the earth that creates seasons and solstices. I talk to a young gay couple, both coming up on ecstasy, who tell me about their polygamous relationship and that 'Sonnenwende' is the German word for midsummer, then hug me.

It's coming back to me – the half-remembered nights I spent, too many nights, wandering dim corridors, queuing for dirty toilets, waiting for the drugs to kick in. The nightlife I left behind is still there. Each weekend, the clubs and bars are filled with new groups of kids from suburban Melbourne or rural Wyoming or Athens or Düsseldorf, students or call-centre workers or rich kids. I'm dressed low-key in black trousers and T-shirt and don't attract much attention. I see traces of white powder in the toilets and my heart aches.

I'm less angular now than I was when I was twenty-five. But as I dance, the beat is shearing off the soft politeness, the regret and sadness, the silence and the longing. I'm not looking for sex or drugs; I'm looking for some kind of completion. It's healing to remember the good times as well as the bad. I'm pleased I'm still able to immerse myself in different environments: the city, the islands, on land and sub-sea. I can no longer have a lost weekend but I can lose a few hours. I can still enter the hatch to another domain and access those disinhibited, euphoric feelings. I want my imagination and words to recreate the sensation of an ecstasy trip: the waves, warmth and wonder.

It gets dark. I get tired. After three or so hours, being sober and alone becomes uncomfortable. It's the shortest night and I always leave early, these days. As I find the exit, I see the couple I met earlier, dancing together with huge pupils and sweat-sheened skin. They don't see me.

Leaving the club is like emerging back above water into a colder brighter world I'd almost forgotten. The year has peaked, the solstice passed, and it's all downhill from here. It's getting light as I collect my bike and cycle home over the Spree. The sky is clear and the road is hard and I am landsick.

VERKEHRSINSELN
(TRAFFIC ISLANDS)

March
Worm Moon

THE DAY WE MEET, FIVE months exactly after I
arrived in Berlin, I buy a bicycle bell. I will ring
the bell all summer.

I think of all the times I've applied mascara and all
the railway stations I've waited at. We sit close on a café
windowsill and my body is alert and buzzing. I look at
him with wide eyes full of hope and seriousness.

*Come sharpen my knives and tighten my brakes. Come peel
my irony, come repair my wonder. Come still my thoughts and
let us sleep sound.*

He expresses himself fluently and openly, in his second
language. He knows how to joke about serious things.

He's a bit older than me and has travelled, growing and building things.

I say, with surprise, 'I could kiss you,' and he says, 'Why don't you?' and the promise vibrating between us in that instant, before I even speak, is what I've been longing for: a flash in the eyes, a dark deep.

He pays me compliments and we go for a walk and a curry and I feel happier, more relaxed and hungrier than I have in a long time. On the way out of the restaurant, we hold hands, easy.

For the next two days – long days at work – I'm smiling, daydreaming and receiving emails before we meet again. I'm excited and a little nervous and I think, This is something. Something real.

After that, we meet almost every night for a fortnight.

I dream of traffic islands. He says, 'I want to kiss you on every traffic island in Berlin.' So we make a plan for the summer. We look at maps. We will journey to islands. We will make brave expeditions into the city, into the summer, into love.

1. Strausbergerplatz

Friedrichshain

Coordinates: 52.518492, 13.428309

Access: Treacherous. Centre of a roundabout, four lanes of traffic, no pedestrian crossings.

Mission Report: There is evidence of inhabitation here: coal from fires, beer bottles and cigarette ends, spent fireworks. Midway along the grandiose Soviet Karl-Marx- Allee, at the start of summer, the great fountain in the centre of the island is being blown in the wind and the evening sun makes rainbows in the spray. Three other couples land on the island while we are there. It is not on the way to anywhere. People who set foot here do so either because the island itself is their destination or because they want to prolong their journey. Traffic islands are for lovers. They are scraps of free space in the city, uninhabited islands, romantic hideouts.

I've spent so long wanting affection like this, from someone I like, and now I'm getting it, and I feel happy but odd. I've lived with loneliness and disappointment, so the messy, active reality of intimacy is hard to remember. How do I participate? I move between fizzing with excitement and thinking, Who is this person in my bed?

When you begin a relationship in your thirties, the stakes are raised. I'm trying to be cool. But, immediately, I have no interest in meeting anyone else from the dating site.

I feel healthy, careful not to lose myself completely: I'm still seeing friends, going on birdwatching trips and to yoga. I apply for new jobs – working with students on a summer programme, and a stint in a bookshop on a Greek island. It's a surprise when I'm successful in both. So, just a couple of weeks after meeting him, I'm flying to Greece, leaving Berlin, and him, for a month.

I spend the month living and working in the bookshop on a clifftop town in the Aegean. I sleep in a bunk built into the bookshelves, above Fiction in English, penned in by Greek History. At night, I inhale flecks of poetry painted onto the crumbling walls.

I am broke and arrive on a cheap flight with hand luggage containing just one jumper that I wear for most of the month, eating the cheapest tomatoes and feta every day, but I'm delighted to be there. I begin to see the lack of certain things in my life – spouse, mortgage, stable employment – at which I often despair, actually allows me the freedom to do things. At fairly short notice, I can spend a month surrounded by books and beauty all day, dreaming of earthquakes, drinking sour cherry juice, tipping volcanic grit from my sandals, sucking the Aegean from my hair, longing for someone far away.

The month is tinged with not only the scent of wild herbs and flowers but also with the headiness of a new romance. It is romantic that, separated so soon after meeting, we are getting to know each other over email, via the written word. I tell him about how, from the terrace of the bookshop, I look down on swallows and swifts performing aerial acrobatics around the houses and cliffs below; about my swims in the sea; about learning the Greek alphabet.

He replies: sweet, urgent and often. I try to exercise caution. Swimming in the Caldera, I look underwater and see the seabed sloping sharply away into the volcanic crater, into a deep blue abyss. It is thrilling.

He is affectionate, eager, idealistic. He reads and looks at everything I have left online, following the trail I have laid for years. He likes all the photographs of me with babies.

Thank you for laying your trail, travelling countries, surviving on minimum-wage jobs, answering all these online dating questions so I could find you in my city.

He finds me a heart-shaped box for my collection on a street in Prenzlauer Berg, the area of Berlin where he lives. He sends me a recording of a pair of owls calling to each other in the forest at night. He tells me that, in the woods, he sees my name spelled in the tree trunks.

I read that one of the symptoms of falling in love is exhaustion. All the pieces of life and emotion and future plans are shifting.

2. Bersarinplatz

Friedrichshain

52.518483, 13.453077

Access: Tricky. Centre of a roundabout, two lanes of traffic and a tram line, no crossings.

Mission Report: There is no shade from the sun on a traffic island, or shelter from the wind. The garden on Bersarinplatz was built specially for the harsh conditions, a rockery of plants that require little soil or water. Wildflowers nestle among thistles and nettles. Explorers are hit by the fragrance of fennel. The island is named after a Russian commander and surrounded by apart-ment blocks of the Soviet 'Plattenbau' style, given new façades featuring lizards. It feels arid, like a desert. I bring two peaches in a carrier bag on my handlebars and we eat them and count magpies as I teach him the rhyme: 'One for sorrow, two for joy, three for a girl and four for a boy'.

I return to Berlin after spending a night on the floor of Athens Airport. I suggest we meet outside, in the park. He gives me a crane's skull he found in the forest. I feel astoundingly horny when we touch.

The German word *fremdeln* means to be scared or shy of strangers but it can also refer to the first contact of lovers after some time without seeing each other. We are taking turns to be daring and cautious: a subtle interplay of shifting power and desire. On our sides with his arms around me, I am happier than I've been in years. Then, I have a fleeting fear that he will change his mind and no longer find me attractive, which alternates with uncertainty about what I'm entering into, then boundless hope, then more kissing.

In his small bedroom, I listen to blackbird chicks in a nest outside and relax completely.

I'm half mad with excitement, potential, sex and surrender. A regular name in my inbox.

Oh, his hands and his mouth and his cock. His shoulders and his voice. In his small room and on my red mattress.

I show him egg and soldiers and Marmite and how to make the perfect cup of tea. He tells me about the German football leagues and the correct usage of different types of knife.

In the evenings, I write in my diary with the book resting lightly on his head, which is resting on my womb.

You are the difference between a pigeon and a dove. You are the similarity between a beef steak and a human tongue.

We email each other sexual scenarios in the day and play them out at night. I cycle from my house in Kreuzberg to his in Prenzlauerberg, the old east, crossing the river and skirting around central Berlin, speeding, exhilarated. Sometimes, I feel unstoppable, as if anything is possible if I'm brave, keep healthy, work hard and am kind. We imagine our lives and then make them happen. I'll ring his bell and climb into his bed and he'll push me against the wall and we'll go deeper.

3. Gleis Insel

Wedding

52.546352, 13.398491

Access: Easy. Pedestrian crossings and Wilkommen *signs.*

Mission Report: This traffic island is a piece of political idealism. Thirty years ago, the island was a dead end, the roads that run around it did not lead to anywhere – they were blocked by the Berlin Wall. The island lies on the edge of old West Berlin, next to a border crossing, just a few metres from the route of the Wall. When this 'oasis' was made, the narrow roads around it were kept open as a gesture of hope that the Wall would one day come down. Care has been taken here with artworks, raised beds, a curved path with curved benches, chess tables and an insect house. The artwork of birds on the island represents freedom: birds are able to fly over national borders that restrain humans.

He says I am a shaman but I don't know it yet.

He tells me that, after I orgasm, the birthmark on the back of my neck flushes deep red.

I say, 'Let's keep doing this.'

On the way home from a bar we hear a nightingale singing in a bush. The *Nachtigall* is much more commonly found in Germany than the UK, even in the centre of Berlin, with an estimated 1,500 pairs in the city. We make a recording and on it you can hear my stifled giggles. The nightingale pauses for a few seconds, as if regaining his breath or gathering his energy, then comes out with another burst of high-intensity song.

He says, 'Let's keep doing this.'

I plan to make a map of the traffic islands as if they are the only land in the city, as if everything else is sea.

4. Moritzplatz

Kreuzberg

52.503633, 13.410587

Access: Hard, traffic is constant.

Mission Report: A perfect-circle roundabout with four trib-utaries to the north, east, south and west. Only by standing in the middle can you appreciate the geometry, looking down the sweep of the roads. In the centre of the circle is a square garden with a tall U-Bahn sign in the middle. The garden contains bamboo. We can feel the U-Bahn rumbling below and the warm summer breeze. We can hear the noise of the rush-hour traffic and sometimes music from the open window of a passing car. Dogs bark. Someone told me that a definition of an island, rather than a skerry or rocky outcrop, is that it has 'enough vegetation for one sheep to graze'. There are no sheep here but there could be – fenced in by the relentless traffic around the coastline.

I hardly ever cry these days. Sometimes, in the morning, he says that I am shining.

My chin's all red from his stubble and my hair's in a permanent knot at the back and it's either like I was never lonely or that remembering how lonely I was has made me appreciate this all the more.

I tell him about my groupie experiences a decade earlier and he tells me about the free-love community where he lived.

I tell myself always to remember the sensations of this moment: hot sun on my skin, the mango ice cream, and

his hand in mine. I'm relaxed, have been in and out of
the cool lake all afternoon and eaten sausages under a
shady tree with friends. We took a cheap inflatable boat
on the water, laughing. The ice cream is tangy and delicious and, after years of cold island loneliness, I know
the value of the hot weather and the warmth of his hand
and the crackling energy between us. I have a good
appetite. It's the first weekend of the summer. I'm happy
to be with him, being sober and in Berlin. The ice cream
tastes great and the sun is warm, and to hold his hand
walking down the street is delicious.

> *I want a tattoo of the route between your house*
>   *and mine, running from my left breast to my*
>   *crotch.*
> *I want a quilt embroidered with your browser*
>   *history so I can sleep in your data.*
> *I want an X-ray of your ribcage.*
> *I want a soundfile of your heartbeat.*
> *I want a live feed of the electrical activity in your*
>   *brain when you think about me when we are*
>   *apart.*

THE WALD

May
Flower Moon

WE MEET AT THE RAILWAY station and he gives me a small torch and a penknife. We travel out of the city, one hour north, into Brandenburg, east Germany, and an area sparsely populated and almost forgotten. Then we get a bus that meanders through countryside and villages: farm buildings, tree-dappled sunshine, apple blossom, storks on nests, his hand on my leg.

I know that I'll always remember the sounds of the forest, *der Wald*, at night. A crane comes overhead, shrieking like a warrior, proud and joyful. A cuckoo calls almost constantly during the days we camp under a 500-year-old oak tree. There are bats in the walls of the farm buildings and we hear their babies chittering in the eaves.

As we walk through the woods, miles with backpacks to get to the farm where we will camp, he pulls me away from the footpath by the hand and I follow unquestioningly. When we are deeper in, he kisses the back of my neck and then we fuck, with me leaning forward against a tree, one boot off and one leg out of my trousers, my socked foot pointing into space. I'm nervous about being seen, but I want him so much all the time. I would do it with him anywhere.

The farm is in a small cleared area in the middle of thousands of acres of national park nature reserve. The owners receive some government subsidies to keep an area grazed by sheep and goats as part of an environmental project. Usually, camping and fires are not allowed in this reserve, but we are permitted to do both in this area.

Before we see the lake, we hear the call of the bittern, a big, secretive bird I've never encountered before. It is a low vibration, almost mechanical, like a bull, or a didgeridoo or a techno soundsystem at a distance, the bass vibrating over the water and through the trees. We don't see the bird but we hear it often, booming, always three times, from the reeds at the edge of the other side of the lake. There are frogs in the shallows of the lake: bubbling, mating, fertile, disgusting, rampant. The noise is something else. We listen to them in our sweaty tent, which he bought from the flea market, and is too small for two tall people, even though we sleep intertwined with our sleeping bags zipped together, turning as one in the night.

On the way, I am attacked by mosquitos. In the tent he counts fifty bites on my back. I am sweaty and bitten. My hands are dirty. I get my period.

We spend three days in the woods with the noises of the night, finding our rhythm as new lovers, boiling lake water to make cups of tea. He cuts wood and chops vegetables and warms me when I am cold. I swim in the lake, stir the pot and gather sticks. At night, we talk by the fire as it gets darker and darker.

Let's learn each other's memories and disappointments. I tell you my dreams before I open my eyes.

We are woken by the dawn chorus, the loudest and headiest I've ever heard: all the birds of the forest, the tits and the blackbirds and the woodpeckers. It feels like we're in the centre of it all. Further away, I hear screeching birds of prey, maybe red kites.

When we open the tent in the morning, we're surrounded by goats and sheep. They had silently got closer to the tent as they grazed. We stay still and regard each other.

The battery on my phone runs out and I don't care. I'm in a foreign country, out of contact, in a clearing in the middle of a vast forest, in a tent under an oak tree with a man I'm falling in love with. I'm elated and bewildered that I've got here.

Our sense of hearing is more alert in the dark. The sounds of the forest speak to an ancestral memory: they touch an unacknowledged desire. I already know, deep inside, about the dangers and seasons and the different types of animals, and coming out here and experiencing them feels like coming home. It's a relief. To be among the bubbling frogs and the shrieking predators and the swamps coming up all around, while in our tent he holds me.

After cooking bacon and eggs on the campfire, we lie together with sunshine on our skin among the trees, then fall into a deep sleep. I wake confused and he teases me, 'Do you know who I am?' and I reply, 'My boyfriend,' and after that he is.

We borrow some bikes from the farm and cycle to the nearest town to get supplies, kissing in a hunters' lookout, kissing in Aldi. On the way back, one of the bikes breaks and, as we're trying to fix it, it starts to rain. It is not easy or comfortable but I like this sense of being really in among it: oil on my hands, rain in my face.

We wash our plates and pans in the marshy lake, up to our thighs in it, in too deep.

This camping trip, all dirty and horny and blossoming, set rolling the summer.

July
Thunder Moon

*W*HAT IS THAT SADNESS SOMETIMES *in your eyes, lover? A glimpse of futility and past pain. An actor's shame.*

There is a heatwave. *Hitzewelle.* Incredible thunder and lightning cracks over the city. I lie with frozen peas on my mosquito bites on the red mattress on the floor. I learn to keep bottles of water in the fridge and my curtains closed in the daytime. The streets are full of drunks and weirdos.

To my delight, he's interested in my island. On Google Maps, we fly over the farm together, pointing out where we could walk, hide, build. After the summer, we plan, we will swap urban islands for a real island and move back to my home. He would like to work on my dad's farm, and I miss the sea.

I'm half getting carried away, half waiting for him to prove himself somehow, when we begin to tell people about our plans. We tell my parents we're coming back together. B says it's brave and romantic and I agree.

There are warnings: rolling a joint at midday, few mentions of family, a default to vague mysticism. I google him, find other lives and names he has worn, other ways he has presented his handsome face. A life is complex, and I realise he's only shown me a small part of his. I'm remaining calm, alert, open-minded.

Everyone has hurts and mistakes and faults. I know how it is to be stuck in a rut.

5. Spichernstrasse Insel

Wilmersdorf/Schöneberg

52.495829, 13.330814

Access: Straightforward, pedestrian crossing at south end.

Mission Report: We see three rats and two rabbits during our short stay on this unusually shaped island. People have placed tubs on the ground to collect rainwater for the animals to drink and the ground is riddled with warrens. Below that, the U-Bahn station. An emergency exit leads

up to the traffic island and we peer through gratings onto
a subterranean stairway. A rotating column advertises
pizza, a further education college and an athletics tourna-
ment to passing traffic. It stinks on this island: human
excrement. This, combined with the presence of rats, makes
it an unappealing place to settle.

I wake up early, with the birds, and lie awake for an
hour or so next to him, deciding I will tell him about
my concerns – about his lack of activity and how he
spends his time when we're not together – and trying
to come up with the best way to phrase it. He wants
to talk more about the island and the farm but I'm held
back by worries.

But his arms around me feel so good that I forget to
tell him the things I'd been planning.

We eat Chinese food outside a café at the busy
junction of Kottbusser Tor, next to phone shops, Turkish
fruit and vegetable stalls and eighties apartment blocks. On
the way home, we stop to watch children letting off Chinese
lanterns, which lift slowly into the warm air, then, when
they're above the houses, are blown gently east over Berlin.

He says that when I'm pregnant he will rub oil on
my belly. He says he saw a blonde little girl in the street
and thought of our child.

He grasps my hip bones in the dark and says this is how he knows it is me.

I'm wearing a blue kimono from a second-hand shop and have cut my hair into a rough bob like when I was a kid. He looks at me with more attention and intensity than ever before. I think this is his heart fully opening but, later, I think he knew it would be the last time he saw my body.

I have lots of photographs of him sleeping. Later, I realise that he was so often asleep.

Now, sometimes, when I hear people talk about 'us', so content and certain, I think, He could leave you tomorrow. I think, You have no idea what's happening in someone else's head.

When I was a kid of eight or nine and visiting a water park, I volunteered to go onstage at the sea-lion show. I raised my hand, desperately asking to be picked. Onstage, the entertainer host told me to jump into the water with the sea lions. I barely hesitated and, brave and excited, ran and threw my pink-tracksuited body towards the pool but, just as my feet left the floor, the host caught me and pulled me back. He and everyone in the audience were laughing. He hadn't actually expected me to jump. That would be a ridiculous thing to do. I was reeling, confused.

I'd wanted to do it. I wasn't afraid. He'd told me to do it. I walked back to my family, humiliated.

His past is catching up with him and my future is calling me.

Summer comes to an abrupt end.

6. Unnamed, twin roundabouts

Lichtenberg

52.539113, 13.539870

Mission Report: The last traffic island I go to alone. I am shocked, with 'he left me, he left me' going around in my head. In deepest Lichtenberg, East Berlin, on the edge of a large crossroads, this island has Plattenbau *and pylons and traffic on all sides. Trees absorb fumes; it's almost hidden from the road. I have a pee, looking for raccoons, with a screaming heart and no one to kiss. I saw this place on a satellite map and came here on the train, past Ikea and petrol stations, car showrooms and wholesalers. No one cares about this land. The remnants of Communism, the loss of a dream. Unpromising places where I find meaning. It's nearly autumn now and the plants are shedding dry leaves. I will complete this project. I will finish what I began.*

He sends me an email that is like an unexpected blow to the head. Our love affair, which I'd thought was just beginning, is over.

After reading it, I'm strangely calm. I change clothes, put on makeup and cycle to his house. If I can just speak to him face-to-face, we can sort this out. He's just got scared. But he's not at home and his flatmate tells me he's gone to the park. I find him with friends, I see him looking relaxed and can't believe he sent that email then came here.

I ask him to explain and for an hour or more we sit on the grass in the park in serious, urgent conversation, chain smoking. I talk and ask and plead and cry but a wall has gone up. He's like a different person. He's decided. I cycle home alone, legs shaking, somewhere outside myself.

I'm furious. He showed no caution when talking to me of the future. He pushed all my buttons and, although I knew it was fast, I fell for him. I didn't stand a chance.

Sometimes, I'm almost high: look at me hanging out my laundry and going to Lidl when my heart has been blown apart.

I fixate. There was a word he said too quietly at the

end of the last conversation and I couldn't tell if it was my name or 'baby'.

After twelve days of no communication, I text *I miss you*. No reply.

I'm blindsided and bewildered by how he so suddenly changed. I can't understand. It affects me physically. There's a salty sheen on my skin and a sour taste in my mouth. I've been smoking too much and not eating enough. My body wants him.

I've given away some books. I've lost weight. I'm spending slightly too much money. But these are only minor forms of recklessness.

It takes some time, but I make the phone calls letting people know my plans have changed.

A traffic island is surrounded by vehicles and roads. They are optimistically landscaped to be appealing when in fact they are pollution-clogged, noisy, unpleasant, unsheltered.

We dreamed of Scottish islands but we were land-locked and urban. Enclosed, we had a fantasy where we could work. We came ashore briefly, on a red mattress, on a little island of a summer, which we made together.

DIGITAL ARCHAEOLOGY

August
Grain Moon

A STUBBORN ENERGY DRIVES ME, DESPITE the hurt and shock, to try to make the most of my last weeks in the city. I have the fervour of the wronged. I will finish the traffic islands project and I will visit more of Berlin's great public attractions, beginning with the imposing Neues Museum.

Wandering the galleries, I am particularly attracted to the splendid gold hat. It glows in its spot-lit display cabinet. It's a ridiculous accessory, a child's drawing of a wizard's hat made real, a solid gold pomposity, the *über*-hat.

The Berlin Gold Hat is a treasure thought to date from the late Bronze Age. It is the best preserved of four gold conical hats from the same period, found in different parts of Europe. The hat appeared on the market in the 1990s; its origins are unknown. It is made of gold sheet and covered with imprinted symbols, lines and concentric circles, and is a magnificent object.

Apart from its splendour, what excites me about the gold hat is that the patterns represent astronomical cycles. It seems to function as a 'long-term lunisolar calendar'. The markings correspond to the metonic cycle, a period of nineteen years, which is a common multiple of the solar year (the time the earth takes to orbit the sun) and the lunar month (the time of the moon's orbit and rotation). By counting and multiplying the symbols, a calendar system can be devised.

The hat bears more knowledge than would be collectable in one human lifetime. It shows up to fifty-seven months and would take many times this to observe, understand and record the patterns in the movements of the celestial bodies. The hat is a way of storing and passing information and wisdom down the generations, and access to this knowledge – the ability to make astronomical predictions – might have made the bearer seem to possess magic powers.

Different archaeological finds have been made on my island. A hoard of silver Viking treasure – brooches, necklets and armlets – was found half a mile from the farm where I grew up. Just along the coast, mysterious stone balls were excavated in a Neolithic village, abandoned at the beginning of the Bronze Age. These precious objects – hat, jewellery, balls – are the things people considered important enough to protect and preserve and they tell us things about the culture they come from.

A large-scale archaeological dig has been under way on the island for the last decade at a site called the Ness of Brodgar. Due to the local climate, work only happens onsite for a few weeks over the summer. The team of professional archaeologists and volunteer diggers are uncovering some sort of 'temple complex' from the Neolithic period, around five thousand years ago. The bones of four hundred cattle were found in the structure, suggesting a huge demolition sacrifice ceremony, when, after a thousand years' use, the site was closed and abandoned.

My area of historical interest is a two-week period at the end of the summer. I remember the details. I had just finished eating a baguette with gorgonzola when I opened the email. The last mouthful was going down. For months now it feels like that bread has been stuck in my throat.

I treat those few days like a crime scene, repeatedly

going back over text messages and emails and phone logs, trying to figure out what happened. If I'd done something differently, could I have prevented it? I've been reading old emails. *I'm building our bed next week*, he wrote, just six days before that email ending our relationship.

In archaeology, stratigraphy is the science of unravelling how everything on the site got there and in what order, through study of finds, structures and contexts. What are known as 'cuts' show where a hole was dug in the past, a point in time where things changed, when deposits were removed.

I investigate from all the different angles, scraping off the layers, seeing if the evidence will fit different hypotheses. He told me he didn't know that his ex was back in town − yet she had announced it on her Instagram. A text cancelled our plans at short notice. There was a long gap before a missed call was returned. In a photograph taken two days before the email, does his skin have the pale sheen of guilt?

Six months after I left, I'm still checking the weather forecast in Berlin. And I'm obsessively looking at his unchanging Facebook page and rereading affectionate, inconsequential emails. I need to stop putting his name into Google. Our physical connection is severed. He sends me no new messages but I cling to the digital bonds. How many times have I scrolled these pages? I am calmed by this surrogate contact. His name dropped off the bottom of my inbox some time ago but I still feel like I'm waiting. I see how many hours and minutes ago he was on WhatsApp and it feels like I'm closer.

I doze for twenty minutes, then wake and look at my phone expectantly. Error messages are given new meaning: *Your connection was interrupted.* My days are held together by cigarettes and repeatedly checking his pages. I'm not proud of myself: I'm aware that my behaviour is unhealthy yet I'm unable to stop.

B told me that fear is the memory of pain but addiction is the memory of pleasure.

I said I'd just have a little look, just peep under the rock, then here I am down on my knees, muddy hands and sweaty face, scratching desperately for whatever I can find.

Many I talk to have their own stories of internet-enabled crazy 'stalking' behaviour in romance. Casual enquiries among friends bring up admissions of hacked email accounts, changed passwords, blockings and unblockings and reblockings, deletions, self-imposed digital exile, fake profiles, impersonations, obsessions and pain.

B, blocked from everything else, used the cycling app Strava to see where her ex had been.

B sent his ex a birthday present and checked her 'last online' every few hours for months.

B told me they made a spreadsheet of the time a cheater took to reply to text messages, trying to find some kind of pattern.

B told me that she still gets emails updating her on her ex's pizza loyalty points.

I want to say, Look, so many of us have done this, it can't be so crazy.

We all have our own online histories, immense data shadows. Searching for him online feels right to me. The technology allows us to fulfil an instinct to seek the people we loved.

I will turn over this rubble. My blunt trowel and dirty hands show how much I care. I'm digging through the strata. There's a sealing layer at the top. Then, between the turf and the natural subsoil, lies the evidence of human history.

And then, there is hitting rock bottom.

For a year, maybe more, I make repeated attempts to stop searching for him online. I tell myself enough is enough. I clear my search history. I move the furniture around in my bedroom. I resolve, This is day zero. And then I mark the days in my calendar: one, two. I rarely get beyond a couple of days.

Why is this happening? First, much of the ended relationship is saved digitally. The communication started on a dating app, moving to emails and texts. All these conversations are still there, the ardour and the arguments, archived, digitised and searchable. I don't know if this is a wonder and a gift, or a dreadful anchor. I don't have the self-control to just leave it all behind and not look, or to delete the conversations.

Archaeologists talk about the 'fill': the rubble and disturbed earth that fills a pit and indicates human activity. 'Spoil' is the excavated dirt that contains no finds of interest.

Second, social media means it's much easier to keep tabs on someone's life, or harder to lose them. Friends tell me that even when they try their hardest to avoid a former love online, they have them come up as 'suggested friends', or in a years-old comment thread that resurfaces, or an old tagged photo. The worst examples are stumbling across an ex's new relationship, or child, when you have tried to avoid information about them. It happens all the time.

Third, communication is so easy: just a stroke of the thumb on this glossy slab I carry in my pocket. The possibility of getting in touch is tantalising, although I'm a thousand miles and six months away. It has a heavy potential. I scratch around the edges. It takes effort not to text, not to call, not to send a picture of my body falling down a well.

A break-up is a grief where no one else, no friends or family, is grieving. Other people have just accepted the relationship is over but for me it isn't over at all. It's like grief but the person is not dead. He's watching woodworking videos on YouTube and logging into Facebook once every two days.

It's a buzz when I see his name appear on my screen. When he sends me the first email in months, my heart is beating so hard I can feel it vibrating through my skeleton to my toes. Is this the unexpected high I'm seeking, an erotic shock? The message is brief and polite, with the crushing send-off *Let me know once in a while how you're doing* followed by *Best wishes*. I desperately hope the coldness is just a problem of translation.

★   ★   ★

I'm watching a video of a white bird, the splendid raptor gyrfalcon, eating the white flesh of another white bird, a swan.

I'm interested in the conflation between the device and the person. On a tech message board someone writes, 'Just over two weeks ago, I developed a flicker', referring to their iPhone. 'You're breaking up,' we say when a phone line falters. In the absence of other communication, I equate the green light of 'available to chat' as the person themselves. B said that the location app enabled her to see where her ex was, then corrected herself: it meant she was able to see where his *phone* was.

I'm digging for something but I don't even know what it is. I'm googling his name, looking for something to heal or hurt me. My digital archaeology leads me to investigate his past. I find abandoned profiles, websites of failed businesses, folders of photographs from parties in different cities fifteen years ago, photos of other women.

Despairing questions are asked by lonely people late at night of Google. There is no reset function on my emotions.

I'm an archaeologist of my own past. I lose hours reading old texts and looking through pictures. Did his words mean something or were they just rubble? I'm curating a museum to our relationship in a folder on my computer.

We speak a few weeks after I leave Berlin and, for some reason, I record the conversation. I keep it, a sad relic, on an MP3 file in the secret folder, and I listen back to it sometimes, often, late at night. We talked on Skype for an hour and a half. He was kind, thoughtful, funny, but steadfast in his decision. When I listen back, I can hear how I sometimes cut him off before he'd finished making his point – carefully, fully, in his second language. I've understood and anticipated what he is going to say and have jumped in with an answer – and he is frustrated. I can hear how we're both painfully upbeat: we're putting on American accents for no particular reason other than to show how breezy and good-humoured we are. We're saying, 'I'm really good', 'That's great', 'That's great.'

On the tape, after I tell him I miss him, there's a long pause. It is the gap where I'm waiting for him to say that he misses me too. He does not. It is this gap I have fallen down for months. I am flailing at the unanswered, the unfinished, the unrequited. I'm lost in the nothing where there used to be something.

I had an app that claimed to draw you in your sleep if you left your phone next to you on your pillow. It somehow converted your wriggles and snuffles into lines and colours. I've kept the neon explosions that are representations of nights we spent together. Added to my folder, a computer model of his dreams.

Will our descendants try to find meaning in our data?

He is the intended audience for everything I post online. I want him to see how well I'm doing – subtext: Wouldn't you like to be with me again? Every tweet or photo I post, I see through his eyes. Look at what you abandoned. Other people respond, and they are poor replacements but, gradually, I lean to internet approval as a substitute for sex, to keep me warm at night. How many likes are equivalent to a kiss?

I need to make a tether to the future rather than carry this weight holding me to the past. I have to move forward. But in the supermarket or walking to the swimming pool, the same glitch repeats and mutates in my mind.

★   ★   ★

I drive to Scotland in new boots and a grey car the same colour as the sky. I drive the length of the country with tense shoulders and arms, hurting. I found the recording he made for me in the forest of owls calling to each other.

Should I meditate? Should I pray? Should I book a workshop in stone carving? Should I write a very sad essay? A very angry novel? A complex, honest letter? Should I cut my hair off, tattoo my skin, start drinking again, fuck someone I'm not attracted to, skip AA meetings, refuse to get out of bed? What if I went in a sensory deprivation tank, or held a stranger's eye, or took a forty-four-day pilgrimage, or swam the Channel, or took ayahuasca, became a Christian, had a baby? Would that work?

The day B unfriended her ex, a year after they broke up, was highly significant. She told me and I understood. The lines of communication were no longer open. Unfollowing, muting, deleted photos, edited histories, ghostings, left on 'seen' for months: we hurt each other so much. Most people know how it feels to be online with an aching heart.

The internet isn't made of stone. As pictures use more memory than text, the oldest cached websites have lost their images. Only words remain.

I want to carve our text messages in old red sandstone. In runes. I want to feel my love with the weight of a megalith. I want to emerge well preserved from a peat bog in three thousand years' time. I want the fingertips of future generations to stroke my wounds.

I drag my shameful folder and bury it under layers in a corner of my computer. I will not, cannot, delete. But I've buried it under a sealing layer. I'm letting the present come in and fill up the pit, new eras, new strata, new dirt.

I grew up among archaeology, overlooking a Stone Age village. Historians unearth evidence of lives in Viking times, the Iron Age, Bronze Age and Neolithic. The evidence is in stone. We still use the stone, re-cycling the same rocks to make new buildings and walls and art. The islands are riven with archaeology, most of it unexcavated. Storms are often responsible for uncovering ancient sites but the storms, seas and erosion also mean the sites are being lost.

I realise that what I fear is erosion. I fear being lost. I'm scrabbling back through time to hold it all together, to salvage. I scroll back months through his timeline. I'm hanging around in the past, up to my elbows in soil and spoil. Where do the jokes go? And where does the love go?

When he deleted photographs of me, I felt

betrayed. He demolished our history, levelled the structure we'd begun to build. I want it to be known and remembered that we were real, that there was something we made and had together.

But it's all spoil. It's all spoiled. A civilisation caved in. The wounds and bones will show evidence of the violence. There was a massacre and a feast and a fire.

GREYLAG GEESE

October
Hunter's Moon

I 'VE LIVED IN BERLIN FOR exactly a year and am booking a flight home for the same date I arrived last year. On my final day, I take the Ringbahn, the train line that runs around the centre of the city, the whole way around, from Westkreuz to Westkreuz, in a leaving ritual encircling the six houses where I've lived, the streets where I've cycled, the places where I've worked – in all the seasons and once around the sun – where I've watched birds and made friends and filled another book with handwriting. The other passengers are having German conversations of which I can understand perhaps 10 per cent, eating bread-based products from paper bags, tapping smartphones, all with their own thoughts and destinations.

With some pathetic pleading on my part, he agrees to meet to say goodbye. I dress up too much and arrive early at the café in the park. He sees the weight I've lost in the month since the email. As he talks about his new job, he is so unaware of how much he's hurt me, not recognising my silent, stiff body language. After too short a while, he has to go and leaves me, alone and dissatisfied.

I sit on the floor of Schönefeld Airport and cry my eyes out, drawing the attention of passers-by. It feels wrong to be leaving the person I love. But the truth is, he had left me. The hooded crows are there on the runway. And, as I leave, hundreds of Syrian refugees arrive in Berlin, many moving into emergency accommodation built at Tempelhof Airport, beside the skateboarders, allotments and goshawks.

I think about sex when I'm on aeroplanes. I remember the different belt buckles of all my ex-boyfriends.

I'd left the UK on 1 October and was back on 1 October. Perhaps I'd never left at all: everyone still in their autumn clothes, going to the same jobs. I could walk into 2 October in the same shoes. The same people are smoking outside the AA meeting, B is still hungover in the same office chair, the Central Line runs east to west, west to east.

B, who had dropped me off a year before, picks me up at the airport and takes me to her place. She drives up the M25 and I am silent and stunned. Here I am in the future and I don't want it. I'm furious. This is not the return I wanted.

Back at B's house, she puts her hand on my back and can feel my vertebrae. I remember her when we were fifteen. I was there for the heartaches of her twenties. She picked me up from rehab at thirty. And now I'm unexpectedly in her spare room at thirty-four. It has been a wasted year. I am back older and poorer, with a broken heart and a botched hair-dye job.

Technology has moved on in London in one year: contactless payment, electronic cigarettes, Wi-Fi on the tube. In some ways, it feels easier back in London. I can understand the language around me; I can decode my surroundings at a deeper level.

I'm not sure where I'm going to live but I'm going to need the car I've just bought from B. First, I must visit the island and my parents.

I drive north and stay with B in Edinburgh, then continue up through Scotland, as my brain and body process the last year. It was a journey we'd planned to do together but now I'm driving it alone. My nerves and body are stretched thin by the last months. My skin crawls and my thoughts are circuitous, as Google Maps guides me further and further north. The roads are clear and Scotland is beautiful but every splendid view makes my heart clench both with its beauty and because I imagined showing it to him.

In Caithness, when the trees thin out and the moor opens up, I get a rush at being, after over a year away, back in my own habitat. I pull into a passing place and have a pee in the grass, then a cigarette, exhilarated by the wide sky and golden evening light.

I catch the ferry that evening and Mum meets me at the pier. I return home just after the first gale of the winter and realise my city clothes are insufficient. I'm drifting, single again, and staying with my mother.

A few days later, Dad picks me up and we go back to the farm. The glimpse of it as we round the bend after the loch always gets me. On the way up the track, we see a sparrowhawk carrying a rodent.

Mornings are often bad. After spending too long on futile internet searching the night before, I wake up and feel like everything is falling away. I cry, wash my face, cry some more, then rub the tears into my face with

Nivea. It's day two again. I have all this love for him and I don't know what to do with it. What people are telling me is that I have to destroy it. I have to destroy something good and beautiful.

But I wrap up warm, go out, work on a drystone dyke – a job Dad has given me – for an hour, on the cliff field. On the stubble field over the wall, a gang of hooded crows.

My fingers smell like soil and stone and I miss you like hell. There is an odd contrast between how people see me and how obliterated I feel by the abrupt end of a love affair. But I keep doing things to help myself recover, driving into the sun, reaching for the light.

I drive familiar roads. Old houses are a year more dilapidated and new ones have sprung up. I admire a dyke beside the road and chat with its builder but my heart's a thousand miles away, somewhere in the internet.

I meet an artist with an easel at the harbour, painting the view. She says the rising and falling tide makes it difficult because the scene keeps changing.

I'm wounded. I left part of myself in Berlin and, on the island, feel like I'm not fully here. I have a quite physical sensation that something is amiss, skin prickling, restless. I put my German SIM back in my phone but there are no messages.

I'm counting days and using magical thinking. Four weeks since I saw him, one moon cycle, in one more moon cycle it will be easier: everyone tells me it will get easier. At times, I want comfort so badly and I think of calling him and looking for it. But it's not there any more.

Maybe I obsess like this because, in my early childhood, my father left often, periods away in a psychiatric hospital, but, crucially, he always came back. I waited and he came home. Some part of me thinks I will be rewarded if I just wait.

I hear the story of the last sea eagle in Britain, an albino female, alone on a Shetland cliff. The birds were persecuted to extinction, leaving just one bird that was alone for years until she was shot by a collector in 1917.

I go out to a smaller island for the Harvest Supper, leaving my phone at home for a weekend. I leave the internet behind. I walk the whole north shore in a cold wind, composing angry speeches in my head. I have a dip in the sea, eat well at the supper, even dance a little but, oh, I am so sad. A seat next to me is heavily empty.

On the North Hill, I climb over a stone stile and drop down into a field, disturbing a grazing flock of greylag geese. I don't know which of us is more alarmed. They are big, loud birds and their honking call is now a familiar part of island life.

Over the last few years, the number of greylags breeding and wintering in our islands has increased massively – from fewer than a thousand in the nineties to 55,000 counted in December 2015. Now, more than half of Iceland's population of the bird can be found here in the winter. The geese have found the land suitable for their needs: with grass they like to feed on, the uninhabited islands and undisturbed hilltops where they can nest.

While other species have been declining in number over the same period, greylags are a success story due to a range of factors. They are well suited to modern land use, especially cultivated grassland, and milder winters. They are also hunted less than they were. Conflict comes as the geese can be a pest to farmers, whose grass they eat and land they trample.

Farmers have been finding ever more ingenious ways to scare the birds from their fields – scarecrows, scarecars, automated booming noises, suspended CDs glinting in the sun, a woman employed as a 'goose scarer'. Nothing works for too long. The birds get wise and return.

Because of the huge increase in numbers, some

out-of-season shooting of the geese has been allowed and, unusually, the meat has been licensed for food and is being sold by shops and restaurants. I buy some goose breast from the local butcher. As I'm cooking it, I trap my thumb in a drawer. The blood and flesh are so similar to the meat in the pan that I become queasy and unable to eat. It's winter and everything tastes like blood and metal, ice and rust.

Like the raccoons, the Icelandic geese are a non-native species that has become successful. Maybe I feel an affinity with the raccoons because I'm an 'invasive species' too. I'm a person of English heritage, one of a dominant culture that has spread across the world. I wonder how much their success should be celebrated and respected and how much discouraged or treated with wariness. The English language is a totalising force, blowing in and trampling the surroundings.

Once a day or so, I have a moment of escape, of relaxation and grace. Today it came while driving, when I saw some people, high on a hillside, flying kites. For a moment I felt as light and fluid as those kites, the nerves and heartache left behind. Then I returned to earth.

There is sun on the hills. Last month, world temperatures jumped by an unprecedented degree. I know that our Western lifestyles and consumption are unsustainable, based on squandering natural resources and the continued poverty of the rest of the world's population.

Any communication with him makes my appetite disappear. My stomach gives a sick drag, my skin tingles, I crave a cigarette. I think of us in front of the big mirror in my Kreuzberg bedroom. He suddenly left but my feelings didn't.

I think about him all the time, counting the days and weeks since we broke up. Forty-five days since he sent that email. I've got my period. The moon is waxing again. Spring is coming. Talk of sex or couples make my heart clench. I can't watch romantic films.

I had thought I was in a love story. I bravely moved alone to a foreign country to find love. My tenacity paid off and I was going home to my island with my beautiful German man. But something went wrong. The narrative of the upwards trajectory of my life was interrupted. I thought that because I was behaving well and healthily things would be okay. What I didn't account for was that other people can let you down.

All that happened was I got rejected. It happens to everyone. It's happened to me before and I have rejected other people. All I wanted then was for them to accept it with grace and fortitude but I have done the opposite: I have raged and cried, argued and objected.

I tell my friends and family that I'm getting over him, that I'm moving on, but secretly there's a part of me that is working patiently on my plan to get him back. I'm reading American 'how to get your ex back' websites. I pay $39.99 for a package that promises to give results. The downloadable PDF guide provides a step-by-step plan to return your lover, starting with a strict thirty days of no contact, followed by an email template: 'be relaxed and unthreatening', 'mention something that triggers a good memory of the two of you together'. I follow the plan and, for a little time, it appears to be working. We enter into contact again and I try not to scare him. I gently suggest that I come over for a visit. Then he disappears, blocks me again. I've blown it.

I won't get better staying at Mum's: I'm going to return to London. This time on the island is hard because I'd planned to be here with him but London is a fresh territory.

As I drive south again into the new life I have worked for, I carry the island and the heartache with me. I'm looking for patterns in the sky and stone carvings and geese. The greylags adapt to changes in land use and not only survive but thrive. I know that others have their own pain to bear. My foot is on the accelerator.

HEARTSICK/LIGHTSEEK

November
Frost Moon

S OMEONE, I'LL CALL THEM B, said that your earliest
memory, whatever it may be, characterises your life.
I remember standing on tiptoe, I must have been only
two or three years old, and stretching up for a light
switch that was just out of my reach. Since then, have I
always been reaching for the light?

The classical elements are earth, water, air and fire,
and this old idea feels right at a sensory level. I start to
think that a combination of two is primal and powerful:
rain on soil, fire in the wind, sunlight on stone. A combination of three is poetry: the sea washing the moonlight
into the cliff, a rainbow.

I'm interested in equinoxes and solstices, the moments

when the planets and the years balance and tip, the instants when we come in and out of shadow. I'm yearning to be plunged into the light, to be warmed and seen, to be illuminated. I'm craving the glow of the moon, which is, of course, only reflected light. I am making my way south again, carrying a slab of grey flagstone from the farm in the boot of my car. I've decided to learn stone letter-cutting, an ancient craft. Stone is the natural material of choice on the island and learning to carve letters and words in stone is a way to link geology and poetry. My ultimate aim is to carve my own gravestone.

I resolve not to search for him online any more, then drive out of London until I reach the sea. B, who has known heartbreak, is letting me stay in her flat by Brighton beach while she is away.

The Brighton stone carver gives me a lesson. The simple tools used are pretty much the same as they have been for centuries, millennia: a chisel and a mallet (or 'dummy'). She shows me some of the most basic principles behind letter cutting: how to hold the tools; how to score the central groove in the letters, then use the chisel to chip away each side. It is difficult.

There is special terminology. I use the chisel to make a 'stop cut', forming the triangle at the end of some letters. The stone can be 'riven', meaning lumpy or cracked. I learn about 'entesis' – the bulge in the column that makes it look straight.

After the lesson, I walk along the sea front and find an AA meeting. Listening to other people takes me out of my self-pity: poor sods in halfway houses, repeatedly relapsing. The man next to me smells of booze, fell off his bike, fell asleep, and his hands were badly swollen and purple.

I still have dreams of drinking. I always wake rattled, and relieved to be sober.

Different types of stone behave differently. The best type of stone to carve is soft and non-sedimentary, like limestone. Marble is also prized. But I want to carve on my piece of Caithness flagstone from the farm.

Alter Schwede ('old Swede') is a large boulder in Hamburg. It has been found to originate from the south of Sweden, 600 kilometres away. It travelled on a glacier in the ice age, 400,000 years ago, and was left. It's an example of a 'findling', a stone out of place.

Back in London, I've found a room to lodge, a friend of a B's place where I'm mostly alone as they work away. I'm in the garden thumping a rock, shards of stone flying. I'm a Neolithic person. I'm a mason. In one pocket I have an iPhone, in the other, a chisel.

All across the UK, including on my island, carved stone balls of uncertain enigmatic use – ornaments or weapons or tools – have been found. Roughly spherical, carved with patterned markings and bulges, they fit well in the human hand. I see in them the most fundamental desire to shape the earth.

I start to notice all the stone carving around me in the city. My walks become richer as I appreciate the work of ancient hands: grand datestones, eroded sculptures, intricate lintels.

In the church cemetery near my house, the gravestones fall into three categories: the oldest have been carved by hand, the stones from the mid–late twentieth century use metal lettering, while the inscriptions on the most recent stones are carved by machine. I admire the craftsmanship on the hand-carved stones, peering nose-to-stone at the regular chit marks inside the letters, each showing a careful chisel blow. They show people making their mark – maybe art in its most fundamental sense.

At a yoga class in the community centre, we lie on our backs with arms and legs in the air, and the teacher tells us it is 'grounding'. I've never understood what this means, just like I've never understood why 'down to earth' is a compliment. I'm slamming into stone. I'm reaching a halt.

I'm fighting the whole time, trying to feel whole, to remember myself. I walk on the common in wellies and my heavy men's overcoat from Berlin, listening to Nils Frahm.

On the common, I walk past a family just as they are sprinkling ashes of a loved one, accidentally stepping across someone else's story.

Occasionally, I make a psychological breakthrough, like realising it's okay to understand that there were differences between us that may have been incompatible and to miss him horribly. These things can co-exist. Or when I acknowledge that it might have been hard for him too. We've both lost something. We both behaved unreasonably.

At the Neues Museum, I saw Egyptian sarcophagi carved with hieroglyphs. These artefacts show what is left after decomposition and time. Maybe my motivation for carving stone is for legacy and solidity. What exists when a solar flare burns out the communication networks? What is harder than a hard drive?

Overhearing a German man talking English in the railway station makes me horny and sad.

In optics, an ultrashort pulse of light is an electromagnetic pulse with a time duration of the order of a picosecond (10^{-12} second) or less. Such pulses have a broadband optical spectrum, and can be created by mode-locked oscillators. They are commonly referred to as ultrafast events.

An ultrafast event is something that's over almost as soon as it's started. Its impression lasts far longer than the event itself. We can never catch a moment in time. We have to surrender to the instant, open to experience it as it happens with no expectation of permanence.

I am frustrated with myself for not being 'over it'. Our affair was only a summer, so why am I still hurting after months? I come to see it is not so much the length of the relationship that matters but its intensity and what it represented. I had been single for years, and the longer I waited the more significance finding someone took, especially since I searched hard and moved countries. Meeting him felt like the prize to my sobriety and effort. Therefore, the blow when it ended was huge and the dissonance ongoing.

One morning, I delete all the social media apps from my phone and replace them with NASA's Space Weather app. The Sun Viewer shows an image taken less than a minute ago, updated every few minutes by NASA's Atmospheric Imaging Assembly Solar Dynamics Observatory. It is dark orange and swirling, with some hotter spots, which appear white, and cooler spots, which appear black. Another concentrates on solar prominences and is bright orange, like a tangerine.

Usually, we can't look at the sun; it's too bright, but in my pocket I have a portal to our star.

I'm still waiting for my first day of the year without weeping.

I google and decide, as many jilted lovers do, bewildered souls, that my ex is a 'narcissist', that he has some sort of diagnosable personality disorder. I read about the pattern of 'love bombing' and 'future faking' followed by 'devaluing' and 'sudden withdrawal of affection', and it all rings true.

At the beginning, the intensity was intoxicating. He cast me as a heroine, a flattering mirror. Once, early on, trying to exercise caution, I gently suggested that he 'cool it' and he exploded: he would not be told how to feel, this was how he was. And after that I didn't want to lose him. Little caution was exercised thereafter:

declarations and plans were made when really we barely knew each other.

He wanted admiration and affection. He saw my weaknesses: my desire for love and a family, and my romantic ideas about the island and the farm. And he made himself into the person who could solve those problems. He saw what I wanted before I even articulated it. I couldn't believe my luck.

B told me it was not surprising it was taking me so long to get over it. When affection is withdrawn suddenly and without explanation, she said, obsession is a rational reaction.

At the cinema, an advert fills the whole screen with a snow-covered hillscape. My entire field of vision is white. The open landscape, the visual release, the light immediately strike me with emotion, homesickness. I'm experiencing the emotional power of light.

He was interested in quick-fixes and extreme trans-formation, get-rich-quick schemes and life hacks. To paint a picture of a dream life can be more appealing than an average reality and it is exciting and flattering to be in this bubble. But you can't live in a painting. Real life takes sustained effort, slow progress and compromise.

Because I wore long skirts and liked the moon, he thought I was a daft hippie, which he liked. As it emerged that I trusted medical science and questioned his platitudes, he began to feel rattled.

A relationship between an addict and a narcissist is a potent and dangerous combination. When the two come together, there's a supply and demand that feeds into both of their particular weaknesses. Narcissists need a constant supply to please their ego. Addicts are endlessly searching, chasing any suggestion of a high. I had so much love to give; I was reckless and open-hearted. He met me and couldn't help but use his accumulated skills of decades to seduce me fully. My big question is if he ever meant it at all.

When it ended suddenly, I had to deal with the shock and rejection, but also the loss of a future we'd begun to imagine together. I am experiencing the end of an intense physical relationship, which I had allowed myself to think of continuing. Babies were whispered into my ear, that my body was his. Now my body tries to reject the new cold reality. My withdrawal symptoms include lost appetite and lost hair, nausea and crawling skin.

But is it unfair to pathologise someone just because he didn't want to be with me? It's just the way it goes sometimes.

At yoga, I move my attention around my body, visualising different areas lighting up: my thumb, my wrist, my elbow. By the end, it is as if my whole body is glowing, vibrating slightly, imperceptibly raised from the ground. Walking home after the class, I spot the gibbous moon above the red-brick houses.

Light has momentum and engineers are researching how it could be harnessed to power sails for space travel. I want to go space sailing, coming at you at 186,000 miles a second.

I wasn't perfect. I have a tendency to see the story rather than the reality, and to overlook things for the sake of a handsome face.

I dream of a single drop of blood dispersing in a glass of water.

To other people it seems easy. I should just stop talking and thinking about it and move on. But the paradox of addiction is that despite knowing the substance of choice is doing you harm you still crave it.

My body is a measuring tool. My pupils expand and contract. I'm always adjusting to homeostasis. I've heard that it takes at least a tenth of a second for the light that hits our eyes to reach and be interpreted by our brain, so in that sense what we are always visually experiencing is the past. Our brains compensate by making a prediction that the present will be very like the past, or the trajectory of an object. I am never seeing you as you are right now, but how you were, milliseconds ago.

All of our senses are subjective and possibly flawed. I am existing in my interpretation of my surroundings rather than a total truth. There may be things here that I can't sense, like invisible frequencies of light and dimensions I can't understand, an alternative to time.

Maybe he was sadder than I realised. I think he really wanted to be all the things he told me he was – and I really wanted that as well. We were co-conspirators in a fantasy. Eventually, he had to confess the charade. It took me longer to accept.

The sun is white, not yellow. It only appears yellow when low in the sky, seen through the earth's atmosphere, which scatters the blue light. The sun doesn't look yellow when viewed from space.

The heartsick do strange things. I saw an event on Facebook, an 'eye-contact experiment', in Hyde Park. I'm trying to find the human connection of a lost lover in a wide range of people. Friends or even strangers. Pain has made me overcome shyness.

I can smell the patchouli as I approach a group of white people sitting cross-legged on blankets. I sit opposite a stranger and, without speaking, we look into each other's eyes for a few minutes. In hers I see at first the reflection of the park – trees and skies beyond – then her blue irises ringed with black. In her eyes I see kindness, and the sadness of a lifetime. And then, in her pupils: myself.

I sit with a young man whose pupils dart curiously, and then a young woman whose habitual smile means her eyes are crescent moons, occluded by lashes. It is like meditation, but instead of using a shrine or a candle as a focus, we are using the point where light enters another human's body, to be converted by the brain into images. It is good to know there are people out there willing to be kind and open, if I can return their gaze.

The winter is passing. I am hurting and obsessed for months and months but there is no way around it.

Stendhal syndrome refers to the physical symptoms – racing heart, dizziness, fainting – that some experience when witnessing a great work of art. French author Stendhal described experiencing them when viewing the great frescos of Florence for the first time in 1817.

To my surprise, twice I am moved to tears by visual art. The first time is a simple lingering shot in a documentary on land art: of light moving across a drystone wall. The second time is when I go to an exhibition of paintings of the island. It is the final day of the show and I decide at the last minute to get on the bus, the 8, to catch it. It is a bus through my past, from Bethnal Green to Bloomsbury. London has changed – Tapas Revolution, Vape World – but I stay the same: smoking at a bus stop, thinking about a boy.

At the smart gallery, I ring a doorbell and am shown up the stairs. I walk into the room, not expecting much, and see the paintings. Before I really register what they're of, I'm crying. Something has hit me, something almost subconscious. The paintings are of cliffs and sea stacks and the ancient stone monuments of the isles. The emotion is homesickness but also something more specific than that. It's the depiction of sunlight shining into the tomb.

It hits a deep emotional trigger in me, of home and simplicity and contrast and power. On both occasions, it was sunlight on stone.

I begin work on the stone I took from home. It's difficult to carve, a bastard: hard and lumpy. My chisel bounces unpredictably. A sedimentary rock, it flakes off in messy layers. But my piece turns out to be interesting: an amalgam of flagstone and sandstone. Chipping off the outer grey layer reveals dark red innards.

First I draw the letters on the rock by hand with a pencil, sketching out the shapes and proportions. I'm not good at this: my centre lines wobble. My letters emerge, rough and wonky, through dust and muscle power and the bang of the dummy on the chisel. My work is very rough, a fine craft far beyond me – much practice – but I must keep chiselling, through thuds and accidents, trying to form a clear word.

Plenty of people dream of falling, but very few ever reach the ground.

The world's communication systems could be knocked out by a solar flare or Coronal Mass Ejection, a solar superstorm, like the one that hit the earth in 1859. Its magnetic shockwave could overwhelm electrical systems. The electricity grid could experience a surge and fail; power lines could snap. On the sun, sunspots can create such pressure that they build up and send out a solar flare. If the internet were to be taken out, if our communication systems were to fail, would we remember how we lived before?

I want to hold and alter the rock with my hands. I want to get down and dirty, into the earth, into the elements. I want to place this letter-carved rock on the ground and then, long after I've walked away, I want my words to catch the light.

> *I want to kiss you wearing a splendid gold hat.*
> *I want to kiss you atop a findling stone.*
> *I want to kiss you in a Neolithic chambered tomb*
> *   at midwinter.*
> *I want to kiss you in the blaze of a solar*
> *   superstorm.*

APOPHENIA

May
Pink Moon

B EFORE I LEFT BERLIN, I painted a raccoon in the
stairwell of my apartment block. I'd been saying I
was going to do it all summer. It was early September,
just a few days after the email, and I was shaky. I bought
paint and borrowed brushes and rolled up my sleeves.
The window was open, it was warm and I was wearing
a crop top, my hair in a topknot, as I stood on the stairs
and painted.

It wasn't a good painting – the perspective was off
and it's hard to make a raccoon that doesn't look like a
cartoon – but it was something.

★ ★ ★

I've never seen a raccoon but I'm making one. I've been hanging around on street corners waiting for them to come to me, but what I've realised is that I can go out and find them. I can make them myself.

People want to help but they want to make it better, smooth it over quickly, and say things like 'You've dodged a bullet' and 'He's not worth your tears.' But if he's not worth it, why am I crying? The friend that helped most was the one who, when I told her I missed him, just said, 'I know,' and sat with me. To have my feelings acknowledged was powerful and I tingled with gratitude.

Other people are unexpected. They all have their own stories, spiralling away from mine. We intersect only briefly, colliding our timelines. They have their own Bs.

I am grateful to B, who let me stay in her flat at short notice and cry in her kitchen. And B, who picked me up from the airport. And B, who just let me talk. And B, who told me the intricate, messy story of her own heartbreak four years ago – I loved every detail – and told me to just hang on.

What helped in the end, apart from time, was to have my story corroborated. Months later, I bumped into someone who had spent time with us in Berlin. When she heard it had ended, she said, 'I can't believe it. I saw the way he looked at you.' She confirmed to me just how strange and brutal it was.

What helped was building walls and swimming. What helped was the earth. What helped was personal symbols and making my own meaning.

Apophenia is the tendency to find patterns. It can be a disorder but, for me, finding patterns is sustaining. Unbidden, certain objects glow with relevance. I find the moon everywhere. This heart-shaped box contains not just a few shells but all the weeks and conversations and regrets of a friendship. We are meaning-making machines. I use all these little personal myths and totems to hold myself together: things to search for when I'm faced with overwhelming choice and freedom.

The week he left me, I burned my arm taking food out of the oven. Over the last year, I've been watching the scar rise and then gradually fade. Now, it's just a silvery dash but I don't think it will ever disappear completely.

I dream I am holding myself as a baby. Me-me says to Baby-me, 'Do you know who I am?' and Baby-me says, 'Yes.' Me-me asks Baby-me where I am, and Baby-me says, 'Everywhere.' Then, we melt into each other like metal.

I resist the idea of learning a lesson from this. This heart-ache is not necessary. It is wrong. I have a wound from which I will never completely recover.

There are things I have learned. Not to eat pomegranate in bed in a sublet apartment. That it's okay to leave parties early. And I see the unlikely possibilities in the middle of traffic roundabouts. And I'm undaunted by menial labour and repetitive tasks. And I'm good at negotiating travel-booking websites to find the cheapest fares. And I'm unashamed of optimism.

At least it ended while we were still at a height of passion, when I still felt excited and blushed when he arrived at my door, when he cycled across Berlin to see me. And I'll always remember that sparkling summer, in my denim shorts on my clapped-out old bike, getting hot emails at work, the cuckoo noise he made when crossing my courtyard, watching the moon pass over the Hof, that rapid hour.

And I remember spring in Tempelhof when, with my binoculars, I skimmed the treeline, the train line, the vapour trails of the planes. I saw a bird perched on an aerial on a small building, perhaps a lightning rod, and when I looked through my binoculars I saw it was a goshawk. I watched it do a large shit, then rise spiralling in a mating display. I was always energised by seeing the hawks.

Things didn't go according to plan. I never found a raccoon. But I came to realise I was never entitled to a certain life, a certain person. I made it all up in my head. And what I have to do now is make up a new story, be brave and strong enough to imagine a different path.

After a few months, I use up the last of my Berlin toiletries, that German body lotion all gone. And eventually, I will throw away a T-shirt he got me from the flea market. I start a new notebook and close my bank account.

One of the last times we spoke, he told me he'd think of me whenever he saw a hawk, which at the time I thought was a disappointing brush-off but now I think I couldn't have asked for anything more.

I never saw one but I know the raccoons are there. There are layers to the city that we never see, different wavelengths we could tune into. There are the postal service, delivery drivers and all the packages being sent everyday, a vastly complicated and functioning network of logistics. There are networks of dog urine. There are bird calls all around, which we can learn and become aware of, at least a little bit. On the street, there are the glances and body language of men, and complex messages about the environment being sent in air pressure and temperature and the markers of the seasons. There are very low frequencies out of our range of hearing. Meanwhile, millions of messages are being sent around us, transmitted through cables by pulses of light. There is still so much to learn. There are many different ways of living in the same city.

I buy a headtorch for night-time walks and delicate jobs and, for the first time in a while, feel excited about the possibilities. My potential territory has widened. I can see into dark habitats, illuminate the creatures of the night, catch a glimpse of them as they go about their business. The places and times I previously thought mysterious and inaccessible are now open to me. If I'm brave. If I'm properly equipped.

I am battered and scarred and alive and beautiful. Wearing the headtorch, I open the dating site again. I have to try a few passwords before I remember the right one, but I barely hesitate as I click: 'reactive profile'.

I realise that, despite the hurt, I don't regret what happened. I'm not sorry I met him. Berlin broke my heart but I'm glad that I was able to let it.

EPILOGUE

Four years later
December
Cold Moon

THE MOON TEXTS TO TELL me it's full. It's 5 a.m., the first morning of the year. I need a wee, so I get up out of the van, moving as quietly as I can so I don't wake my boyfriend and our baby.

We've parked on the moor for the night. Outside it's thrillingly cold and the moon is shining on the snow so brightly that I don't need a torch. It's the full December Cold Moon, which, earlier, we'd watched rise over the hill, lighting some sparklers to celebrate the new year. I look up and thank it for holding me, steady and indifferent.

The last four years have gone in a flash but have also

been the longest, hardest time. The moon continued to orbit; I moved house several more times; the tides rose and fell twice a day; my pain eased. Each month, my body grew and shed and renewed. I moved to a small town where nobody knew me and found new places to swim.

Out there in the snow, I wonder if, in some primal way, our bodies, full of water, feel the gravity of the moon. We maintain an innate lingering desire and it is this pulling me around cities and islands and websites. The location changes but the hunger remains and so does my distant lover, the moon.

A few weeks earlier, I was changing flights at Paris Charles de Gaulle Airport, on my way to talk at a book festival. Maybe it was the perfume I dabbed on in Duty Free that brought it all crashing back, and I thought I saw him standing in a queue but of course it wasn't him, and then I realised I hadn't thought of him for weeks, months even, and now I'm in a future I want to be in, which came in a longer, unexpected way. It's taken so long to feel differently about those times. Suddenly and gradually, a kind of gratitude and grace arrived.

The changes were slow but relentless, like the growing of hair. I didn't notice the healing but one day it just didn't hurt any more. Sometimes there were leaps forward, like the day I moved house and decided, without any anguish, to throw away some small mementos and gifts it had once seemed impossible to part with: the crane's skull, that cheap penknife; the first time I felt a jolt of attraction for someone else. Then there were setbacks: when I returned from a busy evening to an empty house and, still wired on attention and cola, fell back into internet searching for lonely hours into the night, and in the morning felt hungover, disgusted.

Sometimes, it takes a while for the things people say to make sense. He had said, 'This is better for me in the short-term but for you in the long-term.' He knew himself better than I did. He knew he couldn't keep up. He knew I was going to be okay.

And there I was, bright in the sun of the departure lounge, aeroplanes taking off and heart beating. One day, I walked over the top of a hill and didn't look back.

> *Kiss me in an industrial estate.*
> *Kiss me in the city centre pedestrianised zone.*
> *Kiss me in the green belt. Kiss me on the international*
> *date line.*

Kiss me in a sensory deprivation tank. In a hyperbaric chamber.
Kiss me when your face is numb from cold water.
Kiss me in the moments between sleep and awake.
Kiss me in the eight minutes between the sun exploding and us knowing about it here on earth. Kiss me in the eternal after.

My thanks, for the help in the living and writing of this book, go to: Tristan Burke, Fong Chau, Derk Ehlert, Paul Greves, Norbert Kenntner, Lisa Khanna, Theodor Koch, Katharine Hibbert, Karen Hinckley, Mum & Dad, Tom Liptrot and Peggy Desforges, Lisa Mitton, Mira Manga, James MacDonald Lockhart, Diane Northern and Jamie Haigh, Huw Nisbet, Eve Richens, Jo Sweeting, Team Mum, Caught by the River, Creative Scotland, Gladstone's Library, Mothers Who Write and RSPB Orkney. My thanks also to the publishing team at Canongate including Francis Bickmore, Leila Cruickshank, Anna Frame and Megan Reid.

Versions of parts of this material appeared in Elsewhere, Slow Travel Berlin and *Somesuch Stories*. Thank-you to editors Paul Scraton, Paul Sullivan and Suze Olbrich.

With love to Dom and our babies.